Praise for *The Characters of Christmas*

We get to enjoy Christmas only once a year, so let's enjoy it to the hilt! Daniel Darling will help you savor your Christmas more richly with *The Characters of Christmas*. What I love about this book is how Dan helps us get past the Christmas story stereotypes. Instead, he shows us "something wonderfully ordinary" about each person in the story—except for Jesus, the extraordinary Friend of ordinary sinners like us.

RAY ORTLUND
Renewal Ministries, Franklin, TN

An elegant, rich mixture of how almighty God used common people with uncommon faith to invade humanity and display His grandeur. *The Characters of Christmas* provides a fresh introduction to those who helped make Christmas famous. You'll never think of Joseph, Mary, Herod ("The Monster of Christmas"), and the surprising members of Jesus' family in the same way. Several of Dan's chapters would make dinner table reading in the weeks leading up to the celebration of Jesus' arrival.

DENNIS RAINEY
Cofounder, FamilyLife

This book offers fresh insights on a familiar story that will bring meaning to the season.

NANCY GUTHRIE
Author and Bible teacher

One of the most wonderful qualities of Scripture is how utterly human its characters are. People with complex stories of deep sorrow and unquenchable hope are pursued and found by the God who made them, and restored by the Messiah who redeems them. Dan Darling does a wonderful service here to both the biblical text and the reader by mining the details and illuminating the significance of the key figures found in the story of the Savior's birth. Read this one every year.

RUSS RAMSEY
Pastor at Christ Presbyterian Church, Nashville
Author of *The Advent of the Lamb of God*

P9-DXI-017

In *The Characters of Christmas*, Daniel Darling invites us to look fresh at the Nativity story through the stories of the ordinary characters who represent each of us so well. Pick up this book and put yourself in the shoes of Mary, Joseph, Elizabeth, the shepherds, and others, and you'll find your gaze redirected to the One who brings meaning to our Christmas: Jesus.

ASHERITAH CIUCIU
Bestselling author of *Unwrapping the Names of Jesus* and founder of One Thing Alone Ministries

Often the personalities in Scripture we think we know the best are the ones we least understand, most especially the characters of the Christmas stories. Dan listens to their lives in a fresh way in the pages of this book and every Christmas from now on will be better for it.

MICHAEL CARD
Songwriter, Bible teacher

Daniel Darling retells the familiar Christmas story with wonderful freshness and warmth, relating how the characters to whom we point are themselves pointing to Another. This is more than another sentimental reimagining of shepherds in bathrobes and angels with plastic wings; it is a celebration of the glory of God being poured out of earthen vessels that make His grace shine by the reality of how unlikely they are to be carriers of it.

BRYAN CHAPELL
Pastor, Grace Presbyterian Church (PCA), Peoria, IL

THE
CHARACTERS
of CHRISTMAS

The Unlikely People Caught Up
in the Story of Jesus

DANIEL DARLING

MOODY PUBLISHERS
CHICAGO

Edited by Elizabeth Cody Newenhuyse
Interior design: Puckett Smartt
Cover design: Thinkpen Design
Cover illustration of noble men copyright © 2019 by ArtMari / Shutterstock (646858039).
Cover illustration of bearded men copyright © 2019 by ArtMari / Shutterstock (1164512443).
Cover illustration of gold background copyright © 2019 by Phatthanit / Shutterstock (1243028935).
Cover illustration of ladies copyright © 2019 by ArtMari / Shutterstock (1029493684). All rights reserved for all of the above photos.

Library of Congress Cataloging-in-Publication Data

Names: Darling, Daniel, 1978- author.
Title: The characters of Christmas : the unlikely people caught up in the story of Jesus / Daniel Darling.
Description: Chicago : Moody Publishers, 2019. | Includes bibliographical references. | Summary: "Learn something new this Christmas as you explore the oft-overlooked characters behind the Christmas story, like the wise men, Simeon, Anna, and Herod. Characters of Christmas will show you a familiar Jesus from a fresh perspective"-- Provided by publisher.
Identifiers: LCCN 2019022933 (print) | LCCN 2019022934 (ebook) | ISBN 9780802419293 (paperback) | ISBN 9780802497949 (ebook)
Subjects: LCSH: Jesus Christ--Nativity--Biblical teaching. | Christmas--Biblical teaching.
Classification: LCC BT315.3 .D37 2019 (print) | LCC BT315.3 (ebook) | DDC 232.92--dc23
LC record available at https://lccn.loc.gov/2019022933
LC ebook record available at https://lccn.loc.gov/2019022934

ISBN: 978-0-8024-1929-3

Dedicated to Brian Yagoda

Thank you for being a selfless, compassionate uncle,
a loving husband, and a devoted father.
You always made Christmas so special.

C O N T E N T S

Introduction: Jesus, the Grandest Story of All   9

1. Joseph, the Unsung Hero of Christmas   15

2. A Christmas Miracle: Zechariah and Elizabeth   31

3. Mary, the Simple Girl at the Center of Everything   49

4. The Song of the Angels   67

5. Room for Jesus: The Innkeeper   81

6. The First to Know: Shepherds   91

7. Seeking and Finding: The Wise Men   105

8. Herod, the Monster of Christmas   119

9. The Oldest Bucket List: Simeon and Anna   135

10. The Surprising People in Jesus' Family   149

11. The Even More Surprising People in Jesus' Family   161

Afterword: Imagine Yourself . . .   169

    Acknowledgments   173

    Notes   175

    About the Author   179

Jesus, the Grandest Story of All

An old man takes a worn hardcover book off the shelf. He handles the volume gently, careful not to disturb the fragile binding, while returning to his favorite chair, glasses perched on his nose. As he slowly turns the yellowed pages, his eyes rest on the grandchildren who lean in with anticipation. Behind them a fire crackles in the hearth.

It's less than two weeks until Christmas, but at Grandpa's house, these words usher in the official beginning of the season. "Let me tell you a story." They know the story, but they want to hear it again.

And so he begins a December ritual. Each day Grandpa unfolds another piece of the Christmas story. An angel. A scared young Jewish girl. A bewildered fiancé. More angels. Wise men. The kings from the East. The wicked Herod. The shepherd boys in the field. The innkeeper. Prophets and princes, paupers and philosophers, wise men and wanderers.

The kids relish these moments every year. Sure, they love shopping and wrapping presents and rehearsing for church plays, but these moments in front of the fire with Grandpa—this is the heart of Christmas.

Does this rekindle any holiday memories for you? Or perhaps you have your own, equally vivid, recollections of childhood Christmases. For me, three pictures come flooding back every December. I think of my father reading, every Christmas Eve, out of Luke 2. To this day, when I hear the King James Version, I can picture my dad, in a recliner, reading to us, his voice steady and sure.

I also think of Christmas Eve at our church at eleven o'clock. Usually the snow would be gently falling in our Chicago suburb. We'd arrive in our best outfits—a suit and tie for me—and gather and sing Christmas carols. Our pastor would remind us, in a short homily, of why Jesus came. We'd light candles and sing "Silent Night." There was something about this moment every year that evoked warmth and light and hope.

Lastly, I think of that most commercial of holiday traditions gone by: the Sears Wish Book. Before the age of the internet, before you could do your Christmas shopping on Amazon, before Facebook and a million email newsletters delivered all the best shopping bargains, the hefty Sears catalogue, nicknamed the Wish Book, arrived at our house, its pages filled with gifts to stir a boy's longing. The arrival of this treasure was met by joy and followed by earnest searching, dog-earing of pages, and a thousand subtle hints in hopes that my parents would finally, this year, place a rock tumbler under the tree.

I know Christmas brings different memories for different people. For some, the music and the lights and the parties communicate a profound melancholy. Christmas means broken family memories, the loss of loved ones, or aching loneliness. I wonder what your story is this Christmas.

It could be that, like Andy Williams, you think this is the most wonderful time of year; or, like Merle Haggard, you are just trying to make it through December. Or perhaps you are somewhere in between. What I do want you to know, as you begin the journey toward Christmas, is that this season is an opportunity to bring both our joys and our sorrows, our heaviness and our happiness to the One whose miraculous life birthed this season. The good news for both Christmas carolers and Christmas cranks (and everyone in between) is that Jesus came to bring joy to ordinary people like you and me.

✦ **The Light that Illuminates Christmas** ✦

When you crack open the Christmas story, you'll find it populated by now-familiar characters. Some, like Mary, have loomed large on the pages of church history. Others, like Joseph, seem to fade into the background. And still others, like Simeon and Anna, are obscure figures, bit players whom the gospel writers insisted on including in their accounts.

This Christmas, I'd like to invite you to explore with me the lives of each of those people we see around our nativity sets, huddled around the manger and making their cameo appearances in the drama of God made flesh. We should become familiar with them not because their lives are the point of the story, but because their lives, like our own, point ultimately to the one character whose birth changed the world: Jesus Christ. He is the light that illuminates their lives and, if we believe, can illuminate our own.

God's plan was to create a world of beauty and wonder and artistry, a world that He originally created for us, His creatures. He "saw that it was good" (Gen. 1:31). But something terrible happened. Humans rebelled against their Creator and thus brought something into the world that marred God's creation and snuffed out His light. Sin. This is why the world has light, but also is shadowed by darkness and despair. But thankfully the story doesn't end with darkness, but with the invasion of light. The enemy thought he had defeated God, but in the opening pages of Genesis, God revealed His plan to redeem mankind again and bring light into a darkened world.

From the fall in the garden down through the ages, God promised His people that He would send a Messiah, a Redeemer who would be that Light, not only to the Jewish people, whom He had called out to be a light, but also to the entire world. The prophet Isaiah spoke of this day:

The people who walked in darkness
*   have seen a great light;*
those who dwelt in a land of deep darkness,
*   on them has light shone. (Isa. 9:2)*

But centuries passed. God's chosen people Israel continued down a path of disobedience and failure. They were captured by other nations and scattered. But God's promises of a Messiah still held true.

Then, after four hundred years of silence, God's plan of redemption began to unfold. He first appeared to Zechariah and to Elizabeth and promised them a son in their old age. The angel said that their son, John the Baptist, would be a forerunner, someone who wasn't the light, but would reflect the light of the Messiah.

Then the angel Gabriel appeared to Mary first and then to Joseph and shared the news that the Messiah would indeed be born—of the Virgin Mary.

You see, we need for Christmas to be more than just sentiment and gifts and family gatherings. What we truly need is what Christmas provides, beyond good feelings and songs we know by heart. I like what theologian Fleming Rutledge says:

> We can send Christmas cards about love and peace all we want, but the human race is utterly incapable of turning itself around. The children who go to see *The Nutcracker* grow up to be victims of disappointment just like all the rest of us. There is no magical kingdom anywhere.
>
> In a world no better and no worse than this one, at another time and in another place, where men and women struggled against poverty and disease and disillusionment as we do, in a time when moments of hope and happiness and peace were just as delusory and fugitive as they are today, Saint Luke the Evangelist wrote a magical story.[1]

The story Luke (and Matthew and John and Isaiah and others) told is that this baby in the manger was no ordinary child. Jesus Christ was both God and Man in the flesh. And He would be a light not only for the Jewish people, but a Light for everyone. The world is depressingly dark these days—as it was on that first Christmas. But in Jesus, we see the light that dawned and has overcome the darkness.

And there is something wondrous, really, about the people who make up the story of Jesus' birth, isn't there? Something wonderfully ordinary about each of them. Jesus, we see, didn't end God's seeming four hundred-year silence by being born in a Roman palace or Herod's court. The Holy Spirit didn't choose aristocrats or princes to bear, announce, and celebrate the coming of the long-promised Messiah. I like what Martin Luther says about the ordinariness:

Who, then, are those to whom this joyful news is to be proclaimed? Those who are faint-hearted and feel the burden of their sins, like the shepherds, to whom the angels proclaim the message, letting the great lords in Jerusalem, who do not accept it, go on sleeping.[2]

So as we reflect on this Christmas season, I invite you to look afresh at the story of Jesus as told through the lives of those who found their way to the manger, who intersect with the story we tell ourselves every year around fireplaces, in auditoriums, and in hidden places around the world. And let's let the characters of Christmas point us back to the One whose light illuminates us all.

CHAPTER ONE

Joseph, the Unsung Hero of Christmas

Matthew 1:18–25

When Joseph woke from sleep, he did as the angel of the Lord commanded him.

MATTHEW 1:24

As I write this I am about to go with my family to the wedding of one of my former interns. Weddings are beautiful events. The groom stands tall, beaming with joy as his bride walks down the aisle escorted by her father. They grasp hands, they light candles, and they make vows, some with difficult words envisioning faithfulness through difficult times:

> For better or for worse
> In sickness and in health
> As long as we both shall live

I remember my own wedding, standing there as a young, nervous twenty-four-year-old. I couldn't have envisioned then what I know now: a union that will bring us untold joy will also test us in ways we cannot see. I repeated the words "in sickness and in health," but let's be honest. I wasn't thinking of the full implications of that vow. I didn't quite envision emergency room trips, expensive medical bills, and caring for a spouse when they are very sick. And very few who stand and say "for better or for worse" picture bouts of depression, lingering addiction, and aging.

So I watch my young intern tie the knot, I imagine the big dreams he has for his future life with his new bride. It all seems so upwardly mobile, a glide path to success and happiness. Careers, children, houses, vacations, ministry.

And so it was with Joseph in the Christmas story. His longings were probably quite different than the American dream, but as a young man betrothed but not yet married to his bride, he surely had plans. And it was in the midst of this dreaming that his life, his future, and his faith would be tested.

✦ Joseph's Bad News ✦

We don't know exactly how Joseph found out that his fiancée was pregnant, but we can imagine the difficult conversations he must have had with Mary. I love how Matthew sums up all of this awkwardness with the understated phrase "it was discovered" (Matt. 1:18 CSB). How was it discovered? Joseph hadn't yet had the benefit of the angelic visit. He only had the word of Mary, whom he likely hardly knew. Even though they were engaged to be married, the custom of those days was that in the year between the engagement and the consummation of their marriage, the bride and groom spent little time together.

Imagine Joseph's shock when Mary told him that she was pregnant. Unlike today, where sexual activity is assumed among couples in serious relationships, Joseph and Mary had not been intimate. Joseph likely responded with stunned silence. She told him that she was not only pregnant, but that her baby was conceived by the Holy Spirit! Mary believed she saw an angel and may have even written a song of celebration, but Joseph was likely in no mood to party. *Mary, are you serious? How could you do this to me? What do you mean you are still a virgin? That's impossible! Who did this to you? Where is he?*

We read Matthew's account with the benefit of two thousand years of hindsight. We're going through our Advent readings and planning our Christmas calendar. We're putting up cute little nativity scenes and having our kids dress up like Joseph and Mary.

But in this moment, when the shock of his situation hit him, Joseph couldn't see ahead toward what God was doing in the world through his seemingly inconsequential life. This child inside his fiancée may be the Son of God. This child may be the true and better David. This child may save people from their sins and renew and restore the world, but for Joseph, this was his worst nightmare. One commentator says that the breaking of a betrothal like this was considered worse than breaking a business contract.[1] Joseph felt betrayed. He felt alone. He felt stuck.

Put yourself in his sandals. He hadn't seen any angels. He was just faithfully living his life, working as a carpenter, doing his best to build a life for his future family. He trusted Mary to be faithful and devout and had pledged his life to her. And yet, it seemed she had betrayed him.

Matthew says in 1:20 that he "considered these things." Joseph had some serious thinking to do. We don't know how long God waited between Gabriel's visit to Mary and the subsequent visit to Joseph. Was it weeks? Was it days? We know he likely didn't get any sleep in this time of uncertainty and confusion. We can imagine Joseph's fitful nights, pacing, restless, considering these things. Joseph really only had two choices. In those days, if a betrothed bride were found to have committed adultery, there were two options. The plan of action most men would have taken is quite drastic. Joseph could publicly shame her by bringing her before the religious authorities, resulting in the forfeiture of the dowry he paid to her father and possibly even her death by stoning. Consider the case of the adulterous woman in John 8, whom Jesus rescues from public execution. The alternative would be to divorce her privately. He would still endure embarrassment in his community and would face questions of his peers and family for what went wrong, but he'd also be obeying his conscience and doing what is best for Mary. Douglas O'Donnell envisions this agonizing decision:

> On one shoulder Joseph has the righteous requirements of God's Law whispering in his ear, "You have to expose her error. This sin cannot go unpunished." On the other shoulder is the compassion and mercy of God's Law.[2]

Matthew tells us that Joseph was righteous, and he tells us this *before* Joseph was told of Jesus' supernatural birth. He was righteous because he was both committed to following the law—divorcing an unfaithful spouse—and doing it in the most selfless, compassionate way. We don't know much about Joseph, but we do know this: he was a faithful follower of God who would do right when it cost him the most. He would be, then, a faithful steward of the Son of God.

There is much to stop and commend, even in this seeming footnote to the Christmas story. Joseph didn't make a decision out of immediate anger. He wasn't irrational and unstable. For a young man who had just seen his life turn upside down, he demonstrated remarkable grace and poise. He took time and assessed the situation and, seeing the humanity of Mary, made the choice that would be best for her.

✦ God's Good News ✦

We know the reason Joseph didn't go through with a divorce was because God would send a heavenly messenger to visit Joseph—just as an angel had visited Mary. This time, God spoke to Joseph through a dream, recalling a heavenly word spoken to another Joseph. Just as Jacob's son in Genesis would be asked by God to endure a difficult life he didn't envision and to bear the shame of sins he didn't commit, so too would this Joseph.

And see how the angel addresses his subject. He refers to Joseph as a "son of David." God didn't pick just any first-century Jewish man to steward the life of His Son. He picked a faithful son of David. The only other person in the New Testament to be referred to as a son of David is Jesus. This title came with authority, reminding Joseph of his royal lineage and preparing him for the task ahead. This is also Matthew telling his readers that Jesus was a rightful son of David, something Paul later affirmed when he said in Romans that Jesus is a son of David "according to the flesh" (Rom. 1:3).

Then the angel assured Joseph that the baby in Mary's womb was not the fruit of sin, but was conceived miraculously by the Holy Spirit. She had been chosen by God as the mother of Jesus. We don't know how this made Joseph feel. We don't know if he recalled the Scriptures read in the temple and the words of the prophet that described the future Messiah coming from a young virgin (Isa. 7), but just in case, the angel reminded him of the Scripture. Perhaps this reality overwhelmed him, that this "fullness of time" (Gal. 4:4–7) had arrived. The march of salvation history, the fulfillment of prophecy, the long-awaited promise was on his doorstep and in his life. What a holy moment this must have been for Joseph. What a time to celebrate with holy awe and kneel in humble adoration!

✦ **The Rightful King** ✦

It should also cause us to stop and worship as well. This is why we slow down in December and feel the anticipation of Old Testament saints as they awaited Jesus' first advent. This episode in the Christmas narrative reminds us, ultimately, of God's great faithfulness to His promises. Those words spoken by Isaiah and other prophets were not just inspirational tidings to put on holiday cards and Christmas ornaments. They were a continuation of God's promise to send a redeemer, an Immanuel, a God-man to live among us and, to quote the angel, "save his people from their sins."

This is why Matthew opens with such a bold claim that this son of a carpenter from Nazareth was no ordinary man, but was a king, in the line of David, a fulfillment of God's promise. Jesus had to be virgin born in that He had to be free of the inherited curse of sin. As the new Adam, He would fulfill what the first Adam could not do. What's more, He'd defeat the sin and death that so corrupts the human race. David Platt explains:

> In the virgin birth, Jesus did not inherit a sinful nature, nor did He inherit the guilt that all other humans inherit from Adam. . . . Jesus' birth was a partial interruption in the line that came from Adam. A

new Adam has come on the scene, a man who would not succumb to sin. In contrast to the first Adam, in Matthew, a man is born who would save from sin.[3]

Matthew sets Jesus forth, in the angel's words to Joseph, as the rightful King, come to save His people. He is the Creator, recreating and restoring what sin corrupted. What a glorious thought, something worth pondering this Christmas season!

The angel reminded Joseph that this was no ordinary birth and that his role would not be that of an ordinary father. And yet in telling Joseph to name the baby "Jesus," he was reminding Joseph of his stewardship. It was the father who named the sons in those days and, by naming him, Joseph would essentially adopt Jesus. Unlike other earthly fathers, he would not be able to pick a name of his choosing and yet, like Adam whom God tasked with naming the animals, Joseph would be assigned a leadership role in naming the future Son of God. Joseph, son of Adam, would steward this baby who would fulfill what the first Adam could not fulfill.

✦ A Devout Son of David ✦

I find it interesting the way the angel appealed to Joseph in confirming the news of Mary's pregnancy. He first, as we noted above, called him "son of David," appealing to the pride of his legacy. You are of royal ancestry, he seems to be saying to this scared man, you are part of the people of God. Then second, he appeals to him based on Scripture. This is, the angel reminds him, to fulfill Scripture.

This tells us two things about the man who would be the earthly guardian of Jesus: he knew who he was, and he was committed to

Scripture. This is no small thing. This is how the Bible appeals to followers of Jesus today: know who you are as a Christian, and know what the Bible says.

An ungodly person reacts to a difficult assignment by saying to himself, "I don't care what the Bible says, this is how I feel." We may not vocalize it that way, but when we knowingly go against what God has said, this is what we are doing. What's more, we are forgetting who we are.

My daughter currently goes to a public school and is often faced with temptations from her unbelieving friends. I often remind her that above everything, she is a child of God, a follower of Jesus. This not only gives us security in our identity, it comes with a different set of expectations.

And Joseph's response was what you'd expect from a devout son of David committed to the Scriptures: he immediately obeyed. Matthew tells us, "When Joseph woke from sleep, he did as the angel of the Lord commanded him" (1:24).

Immediate obedience to a difficult mission. Contrast this response to the prophet Jonah, who was also called to a difficult mission. Jonah didn't wake up and go to Nineveh immediately. Instead he tried to find a way around God's mission. Craig Keener writes, "Joseph's obedience to God cost him the right to value his own reputation. Many Christians today, probably much older than Joseph and claiming the power of the Holy Spirit in their lives, have yet to learn his lesson."[4]

Joseph was a man of few words. We don't know much about him at all. But we do know he was a man of simple faithfulness. He did the next right thing in front of him. So much of following God is asking, "What is the next right move?"

And let's consider, for a moment, what Joseph was signing up for. This was no easy assignment. In marrying Mary, he would be subject to endless scrutiny. If you think he reacted strangely, at first, to Mary's conception by the Holy Spirit, how well do you think others in his immediate circle would react? Unlike Joseph, they would not have the benefit of an angelic visit. They'd either have to take his word or they'd reject him.

In listening to the voice of God, Joseph was giving up his reputation. Tim Keller writes about the significance of Joseph marrying his pregnant wife in this society:

> Everybody in that shame-and-honor society will know that this child was not born nine or ten months after they got married; they will know she was already pregnant. That would mean either Joseph and Mary had sex before marriage or she was unfaithful to him, and as a result, they are going to be shamed, socially excluded, and rejected. They are going to be second class citizens forever.[5]

By saying yes to God, Joseph was saying no to everything he had worked for, his reputation in the community. It's easy for us to glance over this and not give it another thought as we read this part of Matthew's gospel this Christmas, but we should pause and consider how significant this decision was. Joseph would be a pariah among his own people. He would bear the shame for sins he didn't commit. And yet it only foreshadows the shame that this baby would one day bear on behalf of Joseph and Mary and all who know Jesus. This is why Jesus would later sweat drops of blood in the garden of Gethsemane. Jesus would literally become sin for His people, so much so that the Father, who cannot abide sin, turned His face away from His own Son. He was, to quote Isaiah, "despised and rejected of men" (Isa. 53:3 KJV).

Listen to the way the hymn writer Philip Bliss describes Jesus' shame in going to the cross:

Bearing shame and scoffing rude,
In my place condemned he stood,
Sealed my pardon with his blood:
Hallelujah, what a Savior!

Joseph could bear the shame in answering God's call, and we can bear the shame that sometimes comes with being a Christian because Jesus bore our shame. We can live as outcasts in a world dominated by the devil because Jesus was the ultimate outcast.

Joseph would not only lose his reputation, he would lose his comfort and safety. He would also not be intimate with Mary until Jesus was born. This was not something the angel told him to do. But he went above and beyond what was required in order to say yes to God. Rather than asking, "How do I feel?" Joseph continually asked, "What's the right and best thing to do?"

We learn later in Matthew that once Herod heard of the birth of Jesus and sought to kill Him, Joseph was commanded by God to take the young infant and his wife Mary and leave Bethlehem and go to Egypt. Again, we tend to pass over this detail as we read Scripture. But let's imagine the difficulty of travel in those days: the added expenses, and the severing of ties with family and friends. And yet when the angel appeared to Joseph in another dream, Joseph didn't hesitate. He, again, immediately obeyed the voice of God and went to Egypt. In this journey to Egypt, we once again see echoes of the Old Testament, where another Joseph was summoned to a hard life in Egypt in order to save the people of God and of Abraham and Sarah's journey to

Egypt for food in the midst of famine. This is why Hosea references this history, when he says of God's care for Israel, "Out of Egypt I called my son" (11:1).

This speaks to Joseph's faithfulness and character. He put the interests of his family above his own comfort. I'm sure the transient nature of their early family life hurt his carpentry business. Living as a refugee in Egypt, where he likely joined other Jewish exiles, probably made his life more difficult. And yet even though Joseph was not Jesus' biological father, he was Jesus' earthly father in every sense of the word. He adopted Jesus as his own and cared for Him. This is why the genealogies use Joseph's name to trace Jesus' heritage.

I'm a father in the throes of raising four children. If you are a parent or help care for children, you know that parenting can be difficult. But imagine, for a moment, the difficulty of parenting the Son of God. We don't have much in the Scriptures about what Jesus' childhood looked like. We only have His birth, His travel to Egypt as an infant, and His time at the temple at the age of twelve. But we can assume that Joseph was a father to Jesus in every sense of the word. Even though Jesus was the Son of God, He still, as a fully human young man, had to learn and grow. Luke tells us that Jesus "increased in wisdom and in stature and in favor with God and man" (Luke 2:52).

By all accounts Jesus was an ordinary boy. Consider the way His peers reacted when He returned to Nazareth and began His earthly ministry:

> *and coming to his hometown he taught them in their synagogue, so that they were astonished, and said, "Where did this man get this wisdom and these mighty works? Is not this the carpenter's son? Is not his mother called Mary? And are not his brothers James and Joseph*

and Simon and Judas? And are not all his sisters with us? Where
then did this man get all these things?" And they took offense at him.
But Jesus said to them, "A prophet is not without honor except in
his hometown and in his own household." And he did not do many
mighty works there, because of their unbelief. (Matt. 13:54–58)

Isn't this the carpenter's son? When Jesus began His ministry, it was
His father who was better known than He. Jesus was, in His childhood, defined by His father. It's hard for us to fathom, but Jesus, fully
God and yet fully human, likely learned most of what He knew from
Joseph. The Scripture He quoted when tempted in the wilderness
was probably first heard from the lips of Joseph. The care He showed
toward the weak and vulnerable was probably first exhibited by the
self-sacrifice of His earthly dad.

What's more, it seems that in His childhood, Jesus was indis-
tinguishable from His siblings. That seems to be what people in His
hometown are saying in Matthew 13:55. *We know His brothers and*
sisters. They're nothing special. Maybe I'm reading a lot into this text,
but it appears that while Joseph understood the weight of his calling
to raise the Son of God, he seems to have parented Jesus with the same
care he gave to his other children, who were not divine, who were his
own flesh and blood. He didn't favor Jesus, but he didn't ignore Him
because Jesus wasn't his biological child.

Joseph exhibited the true spirit of adoption. It is a vivid picture
both of God's adoption of us as His children in Christ, but also the
call every believer has in welcoming into our homes and communi-
ties the world's most vulnerable and forgotten. It was Jesus' brother
James who would later write that true religion is defined by care for
orphans and widows (James 1:27). With Russell Moore we can specu-

late that perhaps James first learned this by watching Joseph. "Did the image of Joseph linger in James's mind as he inscribed the words of an orphan-protecting, living faith?"[6]

We can assume, without stretching the story too much, that Joseph patiently fathered Jesus, teaching Him the Old Testament Scriptures, teaching Him to build his carpentry shop, and modeling for his young son what faithful manhood looks like. Perhaps this was one of the reasons the rabbis in the temple were so impressed with Jesus. Yes, His teaching was that of the supernatural. God visiting them. But was some of His recall of the Old Testament due to the teaching He heard at the foot of His earthly father?

✦ Joseph's Legacy ✦

Ultimately, we don't know really what happens to Joseph after he is mentioned in that visit by Jesus to the temple at the age of twelve. He doesn't show up again in the Scriptures, and there is reason to believe that perhaps he met an untimely death.

In every other passage of Scripture where the family is featured, it's only Mary and Jesus' siblings who are mentioned. Given that he was likely older than Mary and life expectancy for a first-century peasant Jew was not great, it could be that losing His father was Jesus' first instance of human suffering.

When Jesus speaks of the way the gospel often divides families, He was speaking from His own experience.

And it seems that there is some estrangement between Jesus and His brothers, who are mentioned at one point disbelieving His divinity (John 7:5) and even calling Him crazy (Mark 3:21). When Jesus speaks of the way the gospel often divides families (Mark 3:31–35), He was speaking from His own experience. One wonders if Joseph were present, would he be the sort of familial glue that could have kept those bonds together? Would he have rebuked Jesus' brothers for their seeming rejection of Jesus? Only the Holy Spirit, we know, can turn unbelieving hearts to faith, but the absence of their father could have played a role. Thankfully, we know that James later believed and became both a leader in the church and an early martyr.

The most poignant absence of Joseph, however, is seen at Calvary, where just before dying Jesus asks His beloved friend John to care for His mother, Mary (John 19:25–29). In this we see Jesus not only caring for Mary's personal salvation and peace with God by dying for her sins, but caring for her personal needs while He was gone. Apparently Joseph is not on the scene and as the firstborn son, it is His responsibility to ensure that His mother is cared for. In this Jesus was following the law that required children to physically care for their parents in their old age (Deut. 5:16), but He was also following the example of His father in ensuring the welfare of those God had entrusted to His care. Both Jesus and James had seen this ethic played out in the life of their father, who exhibited a faith that cares for "orphans and widows in their affliction."

And so this is Joseph's legacy. Barely mentioned in Scripture, forgotten mostly in church history, but remembered by God as a faithful servant. And for most of us this can be our legacy as well if we are willing, like Joseph, to say yes to God.

STUDY REFLECTIONS:

1. *Joseph was an ordinary man willing to be used by an extraordinary God.* God is calling ordinary people to be part of the extraordinary story He is telling in the world. Are you willing to step into the mission of God?

2. *Joseph displayed righteous character in a difficult situation.* In what way are you being tested today? What shortcuts to glory are you being offered? How can you display Christian character in a way that sets you apart in your home, your workplace, and your family?

3. *Joseph obeyed immediately.* When he heard the voice of God, he moved. God may not be speaking to you in an audible voice or through an angel, but He speaks to us through His Word. Are you willing to obey, even in the hard things? What hard and difficult calling is God tasking you with today?

4. *Joseph was willing to suffer reputational harm and loss of comfort for the sake of God and others.* In what way is God calling you to sacrifice personal comfort and loss of reputation for the sake of others in your care and for the cause of Christ?

5. *Joseph took spiritual leadership in his family.* In what ways is God calling to you to spiritually lead in your home and your family? In what ways does He want you to listen to His voice and be an influence toward godliness and maturity?

6. *Joseph is a picture of Christ's shame and reproach on our behalf.* The baby Joseph was to bring up would one day suffer the shame and reproach of the world to save Joseph and us from our sins. Have you taken time today to thank Jesus, our suffering servant, for dying on the cross and paying for our sins and giving us new life?

SUGGESTED CHRISTMAS SONG:

"Joseph's Song" by Michael Card

CHAPTER TWO

A Christmas Miracle: Zechariah and Elizabeth

Luke 1

. . . because of the tender mercy of our God,
whereby the sunrise shall visit us from on high
to give light to those who sit in darkness
and in the shadow of death,
to guide our feet into the way of peace.

LUKE 1:78–79

Everybody, it seems, is looking for a miracle at Christmas. There is something about this time of year that puts in the heart a yearning for something new. Just google the word "Christmas miracle" and you will find lots of results. Here are just a few: a faith-based movie, a Thomas Kinkade collection, and *Reader's Digest* article: "7 True Christmas Miracles That Will Restore Your Hope for the Holidays."

We are all in search of a little magic around the holidays. This is, perhaps, why we fill the season with warm and fuzzy memories and indulge in sentimental movies and music. We do this, I believe, to help mask some of the misery, a way of escaping the brokenness.

However, we know that whatever "miracle" we are seeking, eventually the post-Christmas letdown kicks in and with it comes the return of whatever dark cloud usually hangs over our head—an unfulfilled dream, financial worries, secret health anxieties. Even those of us who know the real hope of Christmas and the real miracle of God coming to earth, in the flesh, as a baby can be caught up in a kind of rootless sentimentality that papers over the anguish of our world.

The theologian Fleming Rutledge reminds us that the hope of Christmas is not a trite expression, but grounded in the reality of a fallen world: "The great theme of Advent is hope, but it is not tolerable to speak of hope unless we are willing to look squarely at the overwhelming presence of evil in our world."[1]

This is why, when we open Luke's gospel and read his narrative of how the first Christmas began, he first gives us a deep window into the heartache and longing of a suffering people. The angels' joy and the shepherds' wonderment come later.

At the time of the decree from the emperor Augustus, it had been four hundred years since God had spoken to His people Israel. Four centuries of apparent silence. The book of Malachi ends with a faint promise of future hope:

> *"Behold, I will send you Elijah the prophet before the great and awesome day of the LORD comes. And he will turn the hearts of fathers to their children and the hearts of children to their fathers, lest I come and strike the land with a decree of utter destruction."*
> *(Mal. 4:5–6)*

That was the last word from God. No prophets were sent to bring messages of judgment or prosperity. No angels. No kings. No deliverers. Israel had been shaken by revolution and war in these years. Most of God's people were scattered among the conquering nations. Some had come back to the land with Zerubbabel and Nehemiah. The Syrians came and savaged the land and the people. Then a revolution by their own Maccabees brought temporary hope—only to be crushed by Pompey the Great, the Roman who brought Israel under bondage once again. Every day as they walked to the temple, built of course by Herod, the ruthless and illegitimate king of Israel, they saw the Roman flag waving in the wind, high above their land.

Yet in the midst of the darkness, when it seemed all was lost and nobody could be trusted, God was silent . . . but not sleeping. The Psalms remind us that the God of Jacob doesn't slumber or sleep (121:2–4).

It might be a little trite to say that "darkness comes before dawn," but in this beleaguered land, amidst a downtrodden people, a new day was dawning. The faint hope of Malachi would be fulfilled.

✦ A Righteous Couple and a Quiet God ✦

Luke begins his story with a dateline. Imagine a newspaper heading that says in all caps: WASHINGTON, DC, DECEMBER 15. But there is more here than simply Luke setting the historical record. Notice the contrast: in the days of Herod, King of Israel, there was a priest named Zechariah.

Herod was the powerful monarch on the throne in Israel, put there by Rome. Zechariah was one of three hundred priests in the family of Abijah (Luke 1:5; 1 Chron. 24:10), one of twenty-four divisions of priests in Israel. A powerful king. An ordinary priest and his wife, Elizabeth.

The news of Israel's deliverer, who would change the world forever, would not come from the palace, but in a Jewish house of worship, to an aging priest.

Zechariah was a common name in those days. There are even multiple Zechariahs in the Bible. But it is not a coincidence that the first words from God to His people in four hundred years would come to someone whose name means "the Lord has remembered."[2]

It didn't seem to the Jewish people living under Roman rule that the Lord had remembered. But it recalls an earlier time when the oppressed people of God languished for four hundred silent years. The God who remembered them in Egypt would now rescue them from their sins. It's not simply that God didn't forget. It's that in God's remembering, He acts.

And God was about to act not only on a national level on behalf of Zechariah and Elizabeth's people Israel; He would intervene in a personal way. Their pain was not just grounded in the brokenness around them, but centered on their private anguish. Elizabeth, like a long line of godly women in the story of God, was unable to bear children. To suffer the indignity of infertility is cruel in any age, but was especially difficult in the first century, when the ability to conceive was seen as a direct sign of God's blessing. At this point in their lives, they'd resigned themselves to their fate. Never would they hear the soft whisper of a child's first words. Never would they walk a son or daughter to the temple. Never would they have the sweet privilege of handing down the story of Israel to a generation of their own.

There is a theme in Scripture of God visiting the barren. Who can forget the despair of Sarah, Rebekah, and Rachel in the line of Abraham, each with their own authentic pleas to God for children?

Or the guttural cries of Hannah in the temple, kneeling before God and begging Him to open her womb, or the bitter spirit of Michal, David's first wife? Luke carefully juxtaposes the righteousness of Zechariah and Elizabeth with their infertility as a way of telling us that the inability to bear children was not a result of personal sin. Then, as now, there is a temptation to use prosperity as a measuring stick of devotion, as if God is a cosmic scorekeeper, dispensing favors based on faith. In every age, this is a temptation. When Job was suffering the loss of his children, the loss of his prosperity, and the loss of his health, tormented in that thin space between life and death, his so-called friends whispered in his ear that perhaps his anguish was the result of a lack of faith. "Remember," they said, "who that was innocent ever perished? Or where were the upright cut off?" (Job 4:7–8). This kind of stuff, they mused, like death and bankruptcy and poor health, only seems to happen to bad people.

But like Job's friends, anyone today who ties faith directly to physical flourishing is wrong. In a broken world, very bad things often happen to very good people. Job was faithful. Zechariah and Elizabeth were faithful. And yet God allowed them to suffer for their good and His glory. Here was a devout couple who, like many children of Abraham under the old covenant, believed God's promise and their faith was "counted to him as righteousness" (Gal. 3:6; James 2:23).

Today as you read this, perhaps all you hear is the silence of God. Like Zechariah and Elizabeth, you are faithful and you earnestly believe God. But all you hear in your suffering is His silence. No cure for your illness. No positive pregnancy test. No new job offers.

From this story you can be encouraged that the same God who

remembered His people in Egypt and remembered His people in Judea and remembered His people on the cross has remembered you. God is not intimidated by the things that threaten you and is working to bring good—to achieve glory—from your pain.

✦ When God Shows Up ✦
(and also why I hate that expression so much)

One of my least favorite phrases I hear Christian pastors and worship leaders say is: "God showed up today!" It strikes me as super flippant, as if God is a lazy teenager whom we are trying to rouse to get into church. My response (in my mind, of course) is always *God didn't show up. He's always here. The real question is: Will* we *show up?* And quite often we sort of domesticate the Almighty by calling everything a "God moment," from finding a parking spot to our football team making a field goal.

But there are times when the presence of God is really seen and felt in a powerful way, and this was the case in the lives of Zechariah and Elizabeth. Zechariah was a priest from the family of Aaron, Moses's brother. Elizabeth was also from the family of Aaron. So priestly functions and duties were in their blood.

There were twenty-four divisions or families of priests, each with three hundred priests. Every division would have two weeks out of the year to serve at the temple, outside of the major festivals, where it was all hands on deck for every priest.

This particular day that Luke describes was a special day for Zechariah because he was chosen to go into the holy place and burn incense at the altar. To decide who would get this honor, priests would cast lots.

If chosen, this would be a once-in-a-lifetime event, the highest honor in a temple priest's life. Zechariah would be the one to offer incense before the Lord at the temple. He had waited his whole life for this. Undoubtedly, among the faithful worshipers in the outer courts were friends and family who came from afar to watch him and to celebrate this moment. After this, Zechariah would be looked upon, like others chosen for this duty, as a spiritual leader among his people. It would be the first or second line in every conversation about him. *He once served incense in the altar.*

Kent Hughes poignantly describes what this special moment might have been like:

> Then came the moment to step into the Holy Place. Before him rose the richly embroidered curtain of the Holy of Holies, resplendent with cherubim woven in scarlet, blue, purple, and gold. To his left was the table of showbread [the bread that symbolized God's presence]. Directly in front of him was the horned golden altar of incense (Exodus 30:1–10; Exodus 37:25–29). To his right stood the golden candlestick. Zechariah purified the altar and waited joyously for the signal to offer the incense so that, as it were, the sacrifices went up to God wrapped in the sweet incense of prayer.[3]

This would not only be a special day because of the incense lighting, but because as Zechariah lit the incense, an angel appeared. If you know the Christmas story well, you can easily shrug and move on. Angels are as synonymous with Christmas as reindeer and mistletoe.

But angels didn't just regularly appear at Herod's temple in Zechariah's day. The people of God, let's remember, had not heard from God in four hundred years. So after this long winter of silence, suddenly and without warning, Gabriel, the same angel who had appeared before Daniel (Dan. 9:21) five hundred years earlier during a time of sacrifice, was now in the presence of the trembling priest, Zechariah.

What do you do when you are visited by an angel? Zechariah's response is identical to Daniel's response: they both fell on their faces in fear. Today when we think of angels, we are not afraid of them really. To be "touched by an angel" is to be followed around by Clarence, the affable messenger from *It's a Wonderful Life*. But in Scripture, when a messenger of God arrived, it sparked fear. Fear because an angel, even in a diminished sense, represented the holiness and white-hot glory of God. In those days, God was not seen as the helpful "man upstairs." He was the One who could strike with vengeance and who judged the nations.

We'd be wise to remember that God's character hasn't changed in two thousand years. Sure, in Christ He has visited us and we can have a personal, intimate relationship with Him by faith. Jesus is fully human and understands our deepest pains and emotions. But He is also God, the One who fashioned us from dust and hung the stars in place. So while Gabriel's words to Zechariah to "fear not" (Luke 1:13 KJV) are instructive to us today—we don't have to fear because God has reconciled us to Himself in Christ—we would be wise to remember that the fear of the Lord is, as Solomon once wrote, the beginning of wisdom.

✦ Silence and Faith ✦

It's more than ironic that the place God chose to speak was the temple, built by an illegitimate king of Israel and often, as Jesus would later expose, overtaken by a corrupted spiritual leadership. God was signaling to His people that something new was afoot; a new day was dawning. Everything up to this point in Israel's long history—the sacrifices, the temple, the feasts and festivals—all would culminate in God Himself descending to earth in human form. The temple and, by extension, the synagogues among the scattered people of God, would no longer be the only place where God met His people.

Gabriel's announcement stunned Zechariah. "Your prayer has been heard." What prayer? Some speculate that this refers to their personal years-long desire to bear children. Others speculate that the angel was referring to the prayer given by Zechariah in the temple, the one whispered by every faithful Jew, praying for the coming of the Messiah. But as I read this, I wonder if the angel might, in a sense, be referring to both. Because both the desire for a son and the longing for the kingdom of God were, in a sense, one and the same. The long years of anguish and darkness, of year after year with no child, likely gave way to a desperate pleading for God to come. There are those requests that we send to the Almighty that seem doable, reachable, and there are those we send with a wrapping of cynicism and doubt, as if the only time we might see resolution is when God fully renews and restores the world.

✦ We pray for peace on our streets, but know only when the Prince of Peace fully returns will we see it in full.

✦ We long for reconciliation among Christians, but recognize true unity will only happen around the throne of God, with brothers and sisters from every nation, tribe, and tongue.

✦ We plead for God to heal the sickness and disease that ravage our loved ones, but understand that even in an era of advanced medicine, our true healing will only come when Jesus returns.

Was this Zechariah's daily heartbroken prayer? Was this what his feeble lips whispered as he lit the incense on the altar? We don't know, but we do know what Gabriel said in response: *Your prayer has been answered.* We don't have to imagine how those words hit the priest. So long had he prayed. So long had he longed. So many years and so many tears.

And now, it was happening, and he couldn't believe it. So the angel repeated the words, this time with more authority: "I stand in the presence of God, and I was sent to speak to you and to bring this good news."

Zechariah, the aging priest. Elizabeth, long past the time of childbirth, would have a baby. Not just any baby, but one that would be empowered by the Holy Spirit in a way that is both reminiscent of the empowering of the Old Testament prophets (Jer. 1:5) and a foreshadowing of the time when God would pour out His Spirit upon all who believe (Acts 2:28) in fulfillment of Joel's prophecy of the in-breaking of the kingdom of God:

> *"And it shall come to pass afterward,*
> *that I will pour out my Spirit on all flesh;*
> *your sons and your daughters shall prophesy,*
> *your old men shall dream dreams,*
> *and your young men shall see visions.*
> *Even on the male and female servants*
> *in those days I will pour out my Spirit."*
> *(Joel 2:28–29)*

John would come in the spirit of Elijah, Gabriel says. He would, like Elijah, call God's people to repentance. John's ministry would be one of both disruption and renewal. He would speak truth (and lose his life for it) to power. He would provoke deep repentance and a turning toward God in Israel. His message would return "the hearts of the fathers to the children" in fulfillment of those closing words from the prophet Micah. But ultimately, this special child would have one job: to point people to Jesus.

Zechariah's response was one of stunned disbelief. It might be easy to confuse his questions with those of Mary, whom this same angel would visit months later and promise an even more miraculous birth. But while Mary's inquiries were laden with trust—*How can these things be?*—Zechariah's response was encrusted with cynicism and doubt.

I'm too old. My wife is past childbearing age. His were not like the hard and difficult doubts thrown at God by David in the Psalms or Habakkuk in asking "How long, O LORD?" (see Ps. 13:1; Hab. 1:2). These were a declaration, like those of Peter when told of Jesus' future death and resurrection: *These things ought not be.* A declaration in opposition to the plan of God. They were like the faithless disobedience of God's people who stood on the precipice of promise and declared to Moses that God could not do the impossible in Canaan.

God loves to hear our doubts, to field our questions, and to hear our anguished cries. But it is disbelief that is a sin, our unwillingness to trust that God can do the impossible. And so Zechariah's punishment was to be struck mute for the duration of Elizabeth's pregnancy.

And in a way, this affliction was less of a punishment and more of a gift from God. To not speak would be to sit in silence before God, to quiet the chattering of the soul and the noise of his circumstances. In a way, this is a work God seeks to do in the heart of all of us. Christmas is a good time to practice silence, to sit and listen to the voice of God, to put away the devices and the inputs that so often keep us from faith. A priest, who often spoke words of blessing on God's people, would be silenced and would emerge with a renewed faith in the possibility of God's promise.

Sometimes God has to quiet us so we can hear Him. Sometimes we have to be still so we can see Him move. Sometimes our words and our busyness get in the way of our faith. They form a cynical shell around our hearts.

✦ Waiting for Dayspring ✦

Imagine the newfound joy in the lives of Zechariah and Elizabeth. Not only would they become parents after decades of infertility and despair and disbelief, but they would parent the last of the Old Testament prophets and a forerunner of the Messiah.

The delight in Elizabeth's life was evident when she hosted her younger cousin Mary after Mary's own visit with the angel Gabriel. When she heard Mary's news—that in her womb would be the Son of God, conceived by the Holy Spirit—Elizabeth gushed with worship toward God.

"Why am I so favored, that the mother of my Lord should come to me?" (Luke 1:43 NIV) she exults. Even though she was present with her own story and her own miracle, she was quick to look past herself and toward the unborn Christ.

I'm struck by this entire scene, described by Luke. An older pregnant woman blessing her younger pregnant cousin. The baby John leaping, in the womb, in worship of the baby Jesus. Here God's promise to Eve was being fulfilled, through the pains of childbirth. A prophet and the Christ child and the dawning of new birth.

Fleming Rutledge explains Elizabeth's joy:

> Elizabeth's cry of supernatural joy has nothing to do with the ordinary human pleasure in contemplating the birth of a child. It is her response to that revelatory kick from John the Baptist, already vitalized by his destiny as "The prophet of the Most High [who will] go before the Lord to prepare his ways, to give knowledge of salvation to his people by the forgiveness of their sins (1:76–77)." No phony innocence here, no sentimental glorification of motherhood, but the announcement of the turning point of world history—the entrance of God himself on the human scene.[4]

This is the real story of Christmas, the heart of Christianity: brokenness and new birth. The same God who birthed life into Sarah's dead womb had breathed life into Elizabeth and Mary. And this baby, Jesus' life, death, and resurrection, breathes new birth into His people.

This theme is echoed in Zechariah's prayer at the birth of John nine months after he first saw the angel. Quiet for so long, now Zechariah is experiencing a renewal of obedience and faith. He first motions with his hands for a place to write and directs his new son to be named "John." Typically, it was customary for the father to name his son after himself, but humbled by God's stunning faithfulness and broken by repentance, Zechariah yielded to the Almighty. Every genuine act of repentance is met by brokenness and obedience. There is always a break from the old ways. No cheap grace here.

Not only was God birthing something afresh in Elizabeth, He was birthing something new in Zechariah and was birthing something new in His people. This is why Zechariah's song, often called the *Benedictus*, is one of the most beautiful passages of Scripture. It reflects the fulfillment of so much longing and desire and the signaling that something new, in Christ, has come:

> *"Blessed be the Lord God of Israel,*
>> *for he has visited and redeemed his people*
> *and has raised up a horn of salvation for us*
>> *in the house of his servant David,*
> *as he spoke by the mouth of his holy prophets from of old,*
> *that we should be saved from our enemies*
>> *and from the hand of all who hate us;*
> *to show the mercy promised to our fathers*
>> *and to remember his holy covenant,*
> *the oath that he swore to our father Abraham, to grant us*
>> *that we, being delivered from the hand of our enemies,*
> *might serve him without fear,*
>> *in holiness and righteousness before him all our days.*
> *And you, child, will be called the prophet of the Most High;*
>> *for you will go before the Lord to prepare his ways,*
> *to give knowledge of salvation to his people*
>> *in the forgiveness of their sins,*
> *because of the tender mercy of our God,*
>> *whereby the sunrise shall visit us from on high*
> *to give light to those who sit in darkness and in the shadow of death,*
>> *to guide our feet into the way of peace."*
> (Luke 1:67–79)

A sunrise, or dayspring, from on high has visited us. This is a new dawn. Quoting Isaiah, he says that "those who sit in darkness and in the shadow of death" would now have light. Zechariah now sees his story as part of God's long story, from Abraham through David. The long-awaited time had come. The narratives of Israel, every single life story from Abraham to Malachi, were only ever small dramas in the grand story of Jesus.

The message of Christmas, then, is not about manufacturing sentimental feelings in vain hopes of a miracle. It's about believing the reality that God has birthed something new in Jesus and because of this, God will birth something new in you and in me. And that newness is breaking out, still today, in the hearts of God's people amidst a broken world. Sinful, dead hearts finding life again. And we, at Christmas, sit in silence and await another Advent, when that child returns as the King, to complete His mission to restore hearts and renew the world.

STUDY QUESTIONS:

1. *We often sentimentalize Christmas and forget that God entered into a time in world history as broken as today's world.* Individually or in a group, ask some questions about the way the Christmas season often papers over the darkness of the world:

   a. *The evil we see in the news every day*

   b. *The deep darkness in our own hearts*

   c. *The way we tell the story of Christmas*

2. **Compare and contrast the visit of Gabriel to Daniel in Daniel 9 and the visit of Gabriel to Zechariah in Luke 1.**

3. **Debate and discuss Zechariah's response to Gabriel.**

   a. *What is the difference between genuine wrestling with God and sinful doubting?*

   b. *How does Zechariah's response differ from Mary's response?*

4. **What are some ways you or your family can "sit in silence" and meditate on the promise of new birth at Christmas?**

   a. *Is there a way to unplug from screens for a few days?*

   b. *Has your family created spaces for rest and meditation among your holiday plans?*

   c. *How are you centering your family life around worship and expectation during December?*

SUGGESTED CHRISTMAS SONG:

"O Come, O Come, Emmanuel"

CHAPTER THREE

Mary, the Simple Girl at the Center of Everything

Luke 2:26–56

And Mary said,
"My soul magnifies the Lord,
and my spirit rejoices in God my Savior,
for he has looked on the humble estate of his servant.
For behold, from now on all generations will call me blessed . . ."

LUKE 1:46–48

Walsh, Colorado, is not just a small town. The next closest town is also a small town. I'm not really that good at geography, but I do have a general rule about the size of a town: when you have to drive an hour to find a Dollar General and another hour to find a Walmart and another hour to find a Starbucks, you know you are in a small town.

Walsh, Colorado, is that kind of town.

This is where my sister and her husband and family live. I visited them not long ago and was just struck by the way life slows down in small-town America and how people (like me) who live near big or medium-sized American cities can easily blow past these towns without thinking and how major media very rarely feature perspectives from this part of the country. And yet in these tiny little towns, there are people going about living their lives, trying to fulfill their hopes and dreams as much as people who live in any major metropolis.

Walsh, Colorado, is the kind of town you only visit if you know someone who lives there, the place that you only see on Google when you zoom in really close. And yet, this is the kind of town in which the angel Gabriel announced the birth of the Son of God.

Nazareth would not have shown up quickly on your map. To get to Nazareth, you had to bypass Jerusalem, the city of David, and the center of religious life among the Jewish people. To get to Nazareth, you had to head straight to the part of Caesar's empire that was the least desirable: Judea. Nazareth was such a backwater that the first thing Nathanael, who would become a disciple, said about Jesus was, "Can anything good come out of Nazareth?" In other words, he was asking, "Why would I be interested in someone who comes from a part of the world that nobody respects?"

In fact, if we could rewrite the Christmas story, this is probably where we'd make most of our edits. You just can't have a hero emerge from a place like Nazareth. And yet here we find the opening act of the Christmas story.

What's more, Gabriel didn't choose to make this announcement to Herod's daughter or a member of elite Jewish society but to a poor, illiterate, unimportant Jewish girl in Nazareth named Mary. As we celebrate Advent this season and as we examine all the characters of Christmas, there is none so unlikely to be at the center of this divine story as Mary. Mary was not looking for prominence. She was, like every other Jewish peasant girl in Nazareth, simply living out an ordinary life in an ordinary town with unassuming dreams. Listen to how pastor and author Kent Hughes describes her likely future, before Gabriel descended on her home:

> From all indicators, her life would not be extraordinary. She would marry humbly, give birth to numerous poor children, never travel farther than a few miles from home, and one day die like thousands of others before her—a nobody in a nothing town in the middle of nowhere.[1]

And yet it is Mary who not only receives the first announcement of the Christ child, but who is chosen by God to bear the Son of God. This tells us something about Mary—her simple faith and her willingness to say yes to God—but it tells us more about Mary's God. We often think God works through extreme giftedness or among those who are wealthy and well connected. But the Christmas story reminds us that God moves in and among those whom society most often leaves behind, that the thread of redemption woven throughout Scripture winds its way through a lot of small towns and seemingly little lives.

Nobody knew Mary's name. Nobody but God, of course. And God knows your name. This is what it means that God is Immanuel. He visits the lowly of station and lowly of heart. He dwells among the broken and contrite. To quote the hymn writer Charles Wesley, Jesus has "come to earth to taste our sadness. He whose glories knew no end."

✦ A Shout in the Dark ✦

To fully understand Christmas, you have to immerse yourself in the setting of Luke. This visit by Gabriel to Mary was so improbable, so unexpected. The people of God were weary and downtrodden. Once a mighty nation ruled by David and thriving under King Solomon, Israel divided into two countries, often ruled by wicked rulers who would both plunder their people and lead them away from worship of the true God. There would be sporadic revivals and periods of renewal. There was even a return to the homeland and rebuilding of their city and their temple. But never would they return to their former glory. All along the prophets promised a coming time when David's kingdom would be restored, when a suffering servant-king would come and rescue them and lead them to peace and prosperity. But it became increasingly difficult to cling to these promises.

Meanwhile, it seemed that the world moved on. Alexander the Great conquered these lands and established Greek culture and language. Then the Romans conquered the Greeks and while keeping Greek culture, also instituted their own pagan practices.

It also seemed that God had moved on. The prophets stopped speaking to His people. For four hundred years it seemed as though God was silent. False claims of messiahs would come and go. A revolt by a family named the Maccabees revived fresh hopes of renewal, only to eventually be crushed by Roman power. Now they were ruled by a ruthless and corrupt governor, Herod, installed by Caesar and distrusted by the people.

So when we open the New Testament and peek in on Mary, we find her among a people mostly cynical about the promises of God. Ruled by the Romans. Divided by sectarian religious tribes (Pharisees and Sadducees and loyalists to Rome). Jaded by the corruption in Caesar's palace and among the religious establishment. Yes, they believed the promises, because this is what Jewish people believe. But would the Messiah come in their time, and would He come to them and among them? Mostly they lost hope.

And yet, in the midst of this bleak midwinter, in the midst of a dark world, to a people who had lost heart, God broke in to announce the coming of the Son of God.

This was Gabriel's second appearance in the Christmas narrative. Months earlier he had appeared to Zechariah, the husband of Mary's cousin, Elizabeth. This was to announce another unlikely conception, the baby who would be John the Baptist, the last Old Testament prophet and the one who would prepare the way for Jesus.

Gabriel's presence is significant. His only other appearance in Scripture occurs in the book of Daniel. Gabriel revealed God's plan for Israel's future destruction and the coming of an anointed one. That anointed one would now reside in the womb of this young peasant girl in Nazareth. Gabriel was God's special angelic messenger, sent to initiate the eternal plan of redemption.

After four hundred years, light had dawned once again on God's people.

✦ "At Just the Right Time" ✦

Mary may have been surprised, but this appearance of angel Gabriel was not a moment too soon or too late. You see, we often view the Christmas story as something that happened—and it did—but it is not a story that just happened. God's visit to a young teenage girl in a small town on the backside of the Roman Empire was planned long ago, before the world began (1 Peter 1:20). The apostle Paul, once a skeptic of the Christmas narrative who had his own unlikely encounter with God, told the people of Galatia that all of this happened "when the fullness of time had come" (Gal. 4:4).

First promised when Adam and Eve ate the bitter fruit of disobedience, God's rescue of the human race weaves its way through Scripture. God called a family and promised that through Abraham, the nations would be blessed (Gen. 12, 17). Then Abraham's family became a nation, whose disobedience couldn't nullify God's promise to send a Messiah. And to David, Israel's greatest King, God spoke of an everlasting kingdom with one of David's heirs on the throne (2 Sam. 7).

And after David, when the people of God were in most distress, scattered and rebellious, disobedient and disillusioned, God spoke a word through His prophets. A new kingdom would dawn, a new King would come, one better than David. And this King would be birthed from a young virgin:

> *And he said, "Hear then, O house of David! Is it too little for you to weary men, that you weary my God also? Therefore the Lord himself will give you a sign. Behold, the virgin shall conceive and bear a son, and shall call his name Immanuel." (Isa. 7:13–14)*

The world may have been asleep. Israel may have been unready. But on that fateful day when God visited Mary, the eternal plan of redemption was right on schedule. "You will conceive in your womb and bear a son," Gabriel said:

> *"and you shall call his name Jesus. He will be great and will be called the Son of the Most High. And the Lord God will give to him the throne of his father David, and he will reign over the house of Jacob forever, and of his kingdom there will be no end." (Luke 1:31–33)*

Think for a moment of the rich symbolism in these words, in this moment. Mary, a daughter of David about to marry a son of David, would bear in her womb the eternal son of David. But more than that, Mary, a daughter of Eve, would bear in her womb the second Adam, who would come to reverse the curse ushered on the human race and the cosmos by the disobedience of the first Adam.

There is a contemporary painting that has become a popular visual icon of Christmas. It's a powerful and simple piece of art. Mary is seen consoling Eve, redirecting her guilt-ridden head upward toward the baby inside Mary. In Eve's one hand is the forbidden fruit; but her other hand is upon Mary's stomach, reflecting on the fruit of her womb who will one day defeat the sin and death ushered in by the first family. Underneath their feet is a snake, who entangles Eve, but upon whom Mary is confidently stepping. Mary's obedience would help lead to the end of Eve's disobedience.

Just as the fruit of the first woman ushered death and sin into the world, so the fruit of a woman would defeat sin and death. As the hymn writer Charles Wesley so beautifully wrote:

Rise, the woman's conqu'ring Seed,
Bruise in us the serpent's head.
Now display Thy saving power,
Ruined nature now restore.

✦ How Can These Things Be? ✦

Luke records Mary's initial response to the presence of Gabriel as somewhat skeptical. This is a natural human response. God had not spoken verbally or through His prophets to Israel for four hundred years. Even though our libraries and bookstores are often filled with volumes about angels and there are claims of apparitions quite often these days, the Bible records very few interactions with angels and God's people. We might think it's common, but in the thousands of years of history recorded in Scripture, there are precious few moments when the winged creatures showed up.

Mary was shaken

And I imagine we would be shaken as well. But what disturbed her more than anything were the angel's words, "You . . . are highly favored!" (Luke 1:28 NIV).

Mary, the young, unknown teenage girl in a small town. Perhaps she was devout and followed Jewish religious practice, but she certainly didn't think she was anything special or worthy of an angelic visit. But again, the angel reassured her with these words:

"Do not be afraid."

You will notice that these words appear often in the Christmas narrative. Whenever angels showed up, people got scared. And that's exactly as it should be. Today we aren't as fearful of God as people were in the first century, and perhaps that's a problem. We refer to God flippantly as "the man upstairs" and treat Jesus as some kind of cosmic running buddy. But in the world of the first century, God's people didn't want God to just show up. Because they knew that if He did, they were not worthy to be in His presence. Moses, if you remember, couldn't look at the face of God and when he returned from Mt. Sinai had a face that glowed like the sun.

God was to be experienced only in the temple and only on certain days and with certain conditions. The people of Israel were aware of their sinfulness and the holiness of God.

And yet the angel repeats that word to Mary: "you have found favor with God" (Luke 1:30). What does the angel mean here? Most of us interpret this to mean that Mary was given a special calling by God as part of His plan of redemption. And this is true. And yet there was nothing, really, in Mary that warranted this kind of special favor. And yet God visited her and chose her to bear His Christ child.

Mary *didn't* say, "Well, of course you'd choose me to bear the Messiah. I've worked myself into this position. I've kept all the Jewish laws and customs. I'm faithful. And, quite frankly, our family fits the family qualifications and socioeconomic markers."

No. Mary knew—and we know too—that favor by God is not earned nor is it deserved. Just as Mary was visited by God, so too we who call ourselves Christians have been miraculously visited by God. We don't deserve God's favor, and yet like Mary, because of the life of that baby, we can be called friends of God.

I wonder if those of us who have called God our Father for a lifetime, who have peace through Jesus Christ, who are promised an eternity in the new kingdom, have forgotten the unmerited favor by which we were saved. Sometimes we feel entitled to salvation and act as if this is a gift that we've merited on our own. Perhaps it's time, this Christmas, to return to the shock and awe Mary experiences when the angel says to her: "You . . . are highly favored!" (Luke 1:28 NIV).

Mary was powerless

Mary's first words were in the form of a question: *How can these things be?* Sometimes we are tempted to confuse Mary's inquiry with the sinful doubt we find in Zechariah, but they are different. Whereas Zechariah legitimately doubted God's ability to have Elizabeth (Mary's cousin) bear a son, Mary was curious in a good way.

How can these things be? In one sense, Mary's question was unique to her. She literally wondered how it was she could conceive a child, having not had sexual relations with Joseph. But on another level, Mary's question is the question of the ages. Abraham wondered how God could possibly make him the father of many nations. David wondered how God could continue his throne forever. And the prophets, while delivering words from the Lord, likely wondered how the coming king could be both a suffering servant and a conquering king, both human and divine.

The truth is that Mary's question is also our question. These things cannot be done by human means. Christmas is not, therefore, a fable, but a miracle. Fleming Rutledge, a theologian, writes this:

> Natural processes could not have brought the Son of God . . . . It is beyond the capacity of human parents to produce a child who is God. Humankind cannot bring forth a Jesus, any more than it can bring forth true and lasting peace. Only God can do it. Only God will do it. Mary was just as helpless as Joseph to make this happen. The human impossibility is overcome by the irresistible power of God.[2]

And this is exactly the answer of the angel. Yes, Mary, this is impossible with mere human ability, but it is not impossible for the God of the impossible. In a mysterious way, the Holy Spirit of God would "overshadow" Mary's womb. This same language is often used in the Scriptures to indicate God's glory, His *shekinah* presence. The God who had shrouded Himself in mystery, who could only be mediated through temples and tabernacles, would now visit the flesh of His people.

The incarnation is the work of God. And while only Mary was privileged to carry the Son of God, those of us who know God by faith in the Son have also witnessed our own miracles. For our own salvation is just as improbable as the birth of Christ. *How can these things be?* we should ask in wonder. How it is that a holy God could offer salvation to wretched sinners? How is it that new life could be birthed in what was once dead?

There is a certain symbolism in Scripture around improbable births. God opened Sarah's barren womb and gave Abraham a miraculous son. God opened up Hannah's barren womb and birthed, miraculously, the future priest Samuel. God opened up Elizabeth's womb and gave her and Zechariah John the Baptist, a forerunner of Jesus.

The point here is not simply that God delights in seeing infertile couples bear children—He does—but that God is the One who brings birth out of death. This is why Jesus often framed salvation in terms of being "born again." He said to the most religious leader of His day, Nicodemus, "You must be born again" to enter the kingdom of God. And Paul, in his letter to the Ephesians, spoke of salvation in terms of God creating life out of death.

The point in all of this rich imagery of birth is that entering the kingdom of God, changing our hearts—this is something only God can do through His Holy Spirit. It's a radical idea that cuts against our man-centered religious framework. We need someone outside of ourselves to save us.

Today people are scratching and clawing to find favor with God. They are looking for salvation in politics, in power, in medication. They even look in self-improvement, even religion. But this kind of work cannot be done by human effort. It's impossible.

The only way to salvation is that the same Spirit who overshadowed Mary now dwells in us by faith and is at work birthing new life in God's new-creation people.

✦ What Mary Was Saying Yes To ✦

At the angel's words, Mary had a simple response: "I am the servant of the Lord; let it be done to me according to your word."

In other words, Mary said yes to God. And this was no simple yes. Let's consider what Mary was signing up for.

Mary was saying yes to bearing the shame of an unwed pregnancy at a time when this carried incredible social stigma. Would her friends and family believe her claims to have been visited by the Holy Spirit? Would Joseph stay with her or put her away? We know the end of the story, but Mary did not.

Mary was saying yes to raising the Son of God. It's hard enough to raise a fallen child, but imagine the burden of raising Jesus. Imagine her fear every time He got a cold, every time He left the home to play with friends, every time He picked up a sharp knife in Joseph's carpentry shop. Sure, God would ensure that Jesus would only die according to plan, but for Mary the responsibility of caring for this most important child would be staggering.

Mary was saying yes to a lifetime of roller-coaster emotions. She'd see Him feed multitudes, raise people from the dead, and walk on water. But she'd also see Him be mocked, jeered, and taunted, even at times by His family and hometown friends.

Mary would have to hold Him close and . . . would have to let Him go. She'd feed Him and clothe Him and rock Him to sleep. She'd see Him push away and grow into manhood. She'd be rebuked by Him at a wedding.

Most of all, though, Mary knew what was coming. She may not have understood all that Calvary would bring, but she knew enough to dread that day her son was unjustly put on trial by His own people, her people. She knew enough to feel the foreboding sense—prophesied by Simeon in the temple—that He'd be beaten senseless, hung on a tree, nails in His hands and a sword in His side. Every parent's nightmare is to see their children suffer, and Mary would live this in the most acute and agonizing way possible.

So this is what Mary was saying yes to. And yet she said yes. Yes, I will do it, Lord. Mary may have trembled when she uttered those words. And yet she didn't have a choice. She gave the same answer all true believers give when visited by God. If this is really true, if the baby in her womb was the Messiah who would save her and all who believe from their sins, then of course she had to say yes.

And today that same question is being asked of people like you and me. What will you say to Jesus? Will you say yes? Will you, like Mary, turn your back on your dreams and say yes to the One who died for you?

Mary could only say yes because one day, some thirty years later, her son would say yes to God. Mary could say yes to the hard call of discipleship because Jesus said yes to the cup of God's wrath in the garden. Our yes is made possible because Jesus said yes to the Father. God would sustain Mary, from a humble teenage girl in a backwater town to mother of the Messiah to pillar of the early church.

✦ Mary's Song ✦

Mary's first response to the news of the angel was a simple yes. But after visiting her older cousin Elizabeth and sharing her news (perhaps the first person she told besides Joseph) and seeing in this godly mentor confirmation of her calling, Mary penned a song, a beautiful hymn that has been sung by God's people for two thousand years.

The Magnificat reads like more than a simple sentimental Christmas poem. It reads like the song of revolution:

"My soul magnifies the Lord,
and my spirit rejoices in God my Savior,
for he has looked on the humble estate of his servant.
For behold, from now on all generations will call me blessed;
for he who is mighty has done great things for me,
and holy is his name.
And his mercy is for those who fear him
from generation to generation.
He has shown strength with his arm;
he has scattered the proud in the thoughts of their hearts;
he has brought down the mighty from their thrones
and exalted those of humble estate;
he has filled the hungry with good things,
and the rich he has sent away empty.
He has helped his servant Israel,
in remembrance of his mercy,
as he spoke to our fathers,
to Abraham and to his offspring forever."
(Luke 1:46–55)

Mary didn't know everything. Mary didn't understand all the angel told her. Mary was, like every other sinner, prone to doubt and worry and fear. But Mary did cling to what she knew. The child inside her womb was no ordinary child.

He would bring "down the mighty from their thrones" and scatter "the proud in the thoughts of their hearts." This child would save His people, including Mary, from their sins. This child would reverse sin's curse. This child would rule the nations.

Mary could look back through the pages of God's redemptive history, all the way back to God's promise to Eve and His covenant with Abraham, and see herself in that story. Mary could see the upside-down nature of God's kingdom, that it doesn't wind its way first through princes and palaces, but among those who are humble enough to receive Jesus.

You may be reading this from your own insignificant place, from the middle of nowhere, from places it seems God has abandoned. But God knows your name. You may be rejected, unethical, or unspectacular but if you are willing to say yes to God, you can know and be reborn by the King of kings.

Mary has a rags-to-riches story, not because Jesus made her famous but because she, like everyone who receives Jesus, was brought from death to life, from poverty of soul to the riches of heaven. This is not only Mary's journey, but the journey of everyone who encounters Jesus by faith.

STUDY REFLECTIONS:

1. *What does God's choice of Mary tell us about God?*
   a. *What does Nazareth tell us about the places God visits?*
   b. *What does Mary's vulnerability tell us about the people God calls?*
   c. *How can we, at Christmastime, adopt a humble posture, ready to receive our King?*

2. *What does Mary's faith teach us about faith?*
   a. *How can we learn from Mary's faith in the impossible?*
   b. *How can we learn from God's choice to highly favor Mary and, by extension, all who believe?*

3. *What does the plan of God, from Genesis to Revelation, tell us about the faithfulness of God?*
   a. *How does Eve relate to Mary?*
   b. *How does the promise to Abraham relate to Mary?*
   c. *How does the covenant with David relate to Mary?*

4. *What can we discern from the supernatural birth of Jesus?*
   a. *What can we learn by tracing the supernatural births in Scripture?*
   b. *How do these births relate to our own spiritual rebirth?*

5. What can we learn from Mary's "yes" to God?

   a. *How was Mary able to say yes?*

   b. *How are we able to say yes?*

   c. *How does the call of Mary to obedience differ from many of today's appeals to faith?*

SUGGESTED CHRISTMAS SONGS:

"Mary, Did You Know?" by Mark Lowry

"What Her Heart Remembered" by Michael Card

CHAPTER FOUR

The Song of the Angels

Luke 2:13-14

*And suddenly there was with the angel
a multitude of the heavenly host praising God and saying,
"Glory to God in the highest, and on earth peace
among those with whom he is pleased!"*

LUKE 2:13–14

There is one character—or rather, a series of characters—hovering over the Christmas story. Literally. They are not quite human, but not quite divine, and sometimes they seem to float in the background and at other times, they come to the fore, announcing the good news of the birth of Jesus. We cannot step into any of the incarnation narratives in Scripture without running into them: the angels.

An angel named Gabriel first shows up in the temple while a stunned priest named Zechariah is minding his own business lighting the incense on the altar (Luke 1:11–19). As Zechariah trembles, dumbfounded, the angel announces that Zechariah's wife, Elizabeth, would soon conceive a special, Elijah-like son.

A few months later, Gabriel shows up in the home of a poor teenager named Mary. Here the angel announces an even more impossible conception: a child by this young virgin who would be, gulp, the Son of God.

And not once, but twice, an angel was sent to reassure Mary's not-so-sure husband that this conception was indeed of God and not the result of her infidelity (proving that sometimes husbands require angels to work overtime.)

Angels were the ones who filled a normally quiet Bethlehem sky one night, hovering above a shepherd's field, announcing to these lowly men that something big and extraordinary was happening in their sleepy town. The first Christmas pageant was not written by songwriters in Nashville, but by messengers from heaven.

Angels didn't just announce good news. They were also sent by God to protect the baby King from an illegitimate and ruthless king. An angel disturbed the sleep of the magi and redirected their journey, thwarting a ruthless Herod from ending the life of the life-giver. An angel also came to Joseph a third time—imagine how hard it would be for him to get a full night's sleep after this—and told him to pack his family and get to Egypt, escaping Herod's sword.

You can't tell the story of Christmas without the angels.

✦ Witnesses to Redemption ✦

What would it look like for us to zoom out a bit and view Jesus' birth from their vantage point? To climb this summit, we have to travel back before that not-so-silent night in Bethlehem, before Gabriel's appearance in the temple, even back before Genesis. The Bible tells us that angels were present at the dawn of creation (Job 38:7) and have held a courtside seat to the unfolding of God's majestic plan of redemption.

There is a lot of mystery around these beings, but we do know that angels were created by and for Christ (Col. 1:16). Spirits (Heb. 1:14) who, at times, don human form to accomplish earthly missions, cannot reproduce and, unlike humans, do not die (Luke 20:36). And also unlike humans, they seem to have supernatural power. (In Revelation 10:2, one massive angel has a foot on the sea and a foot on the land.) Angels also seem to have emotion, intellect, and will.

How many angels are there in the world? We don't really know. The writer of Hebrews says they cannot be numbered (Heb. 12:22), and in other places they are counted in the thousands and thousands (Ps. 68:17; Rev. 5:11). Angels serve a variety of roles in Scripture: they advocate, they protect, they make war, they announce, they teach, they comfort, and they guide. But mostly, these heavenly messengers have one job: to worship the triune God.

Scripture is not totally clear about when angels were created, but most scholars and theologians in church history have believed that before God created the world, there was a cosmic battle in heaven. Lucifer, the highest angel, beautiful and gifted, created to reflect God's beauty, lifted himself up against the Almighty (Isa. 14:12–17). The Bible says that a third of the angels sided with Lucifer (Rev. 12:4). And so Lucifer and his demons became God's sworn enemies.

But be assured that this was not an equal battle between two heavyweights. The book of Job peels back the curtain and reminds us that even when Satan, a created being, commits evil, he is only allowed to do what God allows in His mysterious will. God would demonstrate His glory in the universe by ultimately defeating the enemy. God was not shaken by Lucifer's fall.

The angels were witnesses to God's creation of the world, watching with wonder as the Trinity formed the universe with His spoken word (Gen. 1; Job 38). Varied species of animals, plants fitting into God's perfect ecosystem of beauty, the artist of heaven swabbing His creative brush across the universe. At each level of mastery, they heard God declare about His work: "This is good."

But in the midst of God's spectacular new work there was something missing. The canvas of creation was incomplete. And thus the divine pause. This is where I imagine the angels gasping in amazement. God had not made the earth as an untouched museum piece, but as its own kind of studio. The earth needed a new and special kind of beings, artists who reflect their Creator but also take up the new instruments of creation and do their own creating. So the Godhead speaks, "Let us"—notice the intentional deliberation from all members of the Trinity—"make man."

Moses, the author of Genesis, narrates the crafting of human life with such rich language, describing God reaching down into His new world to grasp a handful of dust. From this fresh dirt, the Creator sculpts a man and into this man, He softly breathes life into the first human. From this flesh and blood, God sculpts a woman and again forms flesh and blood and sinew. Humans would be a new and distinct kind of creature.

Humans would have souls. Humans would have spirits. Humans would be made in the . . . *imago Dei.* In God's image.

At all of this, we know, the angels spontaneously rejoiced. Job tells us about the concert in heaven that erupted at creation: "the morning stars sang together and all the sons of God shouted for joy" (Job 38:7).

From the angels' perspective this was both a glorious moment and a divine risk. God needed no intimacy with another kind of being to find fulfillment in Himself. For eternity, the Father, Son, and Spirit communed with uninterrupted intimacy. And every other part of creation would forever stoop to worship the Creator, but this new kind of being could both love God—and could also reject God.

What, they wonder, is God up to? They ponder this as they guard the entrance to Eden and watch as God and man commune in innocence. The man and woman enjoying each other and walking in union with God. They begin the stewardship of God's new world.

But lurking, the angels know, is an enemy. Satan doesn't find joy in the intimacy God enjoys with His image bearers. So the father of lies inhabits a serpent and begins his slow work of deception.

The angels watch. It would make no sense, would it? Why would humans choose the serpent over the Creator of snakes? Why would they believe the lie that the One who created them was holding out, was keeping back joy?

Yet it happens. And this new and beautiful world turns dark. Sin begins its slow and sure decay, marbling death into every sliver of God's beautiful world. God's image bearers have made a destructive alliance with the enemy and are thrust out of Eden.

The angels are aware of God's attributes. They know He is not surprised by anything. And so they watch to see how God's glory will be revealed, even in this tragic turn of events. They listen in on God's words of judgment and hope (Gen. 3:15).

Angels watch in wonder as God unfolds history.

Angels watch in wonder as God unfolds history. They see the

work of Satan as he assumes control as prince and power of the air. And they see and engage in God's unfolding plan to rescue His beloved creation. And it's a twisting, often agonizing story with only small light rays of redemption.

The angels watch sin overwhelm the human race with corruption while God rescues and restores through the single faithful family of Noah.

The angels observe God pursue an idol-worshiping pagan named Abraham, who follows with threadbare faith into a journey unknown. Out of Abraham He builds a people, who at times follow and at times flout His direction. From this nation He plucks and crowns an obscure shepherd boy, the least of his brethren. From this fragile warrior-king would emerge the seeds of a new kingdom, bigger than Israel.

But the angels also see the dark fingerprints of Satan. Generation after generation, the people of God face both foes internal and external. Cycles of idolatry and repentance lead, eventually, to the judgment of conquerors. Kings and queens channel the spirit of Lucifer and attempt to snuff out the promise, but God keeps His promise and preserves a remnant. The angels listen as the prophets warn of judgment but promise a future King and kingdom, one in which the curse of Eden will be folded back and God will do a new thing.

They watch as God scatters Israel to the nations and gathers a remnant back in the land. But when the final prophet speaks, silence fills the centuries. God's people become pawns as the nations war. False messiahs appear on the scene, teasing a weary and cynical people with faint and false salvation.

And then, they are summoned, first Gabriel, to announce a new thing. They can hardly believe or understand what is about to unfold.

The Creator wouldn't just rescue His creation. The Son would become . . . human. And He wouldn't appear in dazzling robes and white-hot splendor. He wouldn't blind eyes like on Sinai or boom from heaven like in Eden. God would enter the world as a vulnerable, dependent, fragile baby.

So they announce to Zechariah and Mary and Joseph. They flood the earth with a celebration to the shepherds. They warn the magi.

The angels were also on call as Jesus grew. In His hour of temptation, they refreshed Him as He proved the second Adam would flourish where the first Adam failed. They strengthened Jesus as He accepted the Father's cup in the garden. They were absent—at Jesus' request—when they could have been summoned as an army to sweep away the Roman executioners. And, in white robes, they sat atop the stone, wondering and watching as the first visitors struggled to understand the meaning of Jesus' empty tomb. The angels knew He would rise. The angels knew the power of God over sin, death, and the grave.

This was the end of Jesus' earthly ministry, but not the end of His work. As He ascended, they chastened the puzzled disciples. This same Jesus would return in power one day. So go, they said, and tell the world!

And go these previously fearful men went, throughout Israel and eventually around the known world. They saw the Spirit of God descend and birth a movement out of a fledgling band of disciples. At times they were summoned to action: freeing the apostles from prison, sending Philip on an evangelistic assignment, appearing to a Roman Gentile, Cornelius, as a sign of the gospel's spread to the nations, releasing Peter from prison, and taking the life of the wicked king Herod, who had the brother of Jesus killed.

The angels watched, in amazement, as Jesus transformed Saul from persecutor to pitchman, and an angel guided this messenger to the Gentiles through shipwreck and into Caesar's court.

We last see the angel traveling to the remote Isle of Patmos, narrating a vision of the end of the age to the last remaining apostle. John's revelation shows the angels leading the New Jerusalem in worship, as every nation and tribe gathers around the throne of God. "Holy, Holy," they declare, "is the Lord God Almighty, who was and is and is to come" (Rev. 4:8).

✦ Hearing the Angels ✦

Let's travel back to that night in Bethlehem under the stars, to the shepherds' fields, the quiet punctuated by the occasional bleating of sheep. To the rest of the world, from the marbled halls of Rome to Herod's palace, this was just an ordinary night. It was a time of peace in the Roman Empire. History was, it seemed, running on an even plain.

But the angels knew. They knew that this was, to quote Galatians, "when the fullness of time had come." All of human history funneled toward this moment. A baby was born in a cave in the nearby village. Few knew. Few cared. Babies are born every minute of every day around the world.

The angels knew, though, that this was something. The same Creator who breathed life into humans would breathe His first breath in subjection to the world He made. This was not Jesus pretending to be a baby.

The angels' song was just the beginning of an ongoing chorus of creativity. The incarnation stirs in us some of the most beautiful worship: Mary's *Magnificat*, Elizabeth's *Beatitude*, Zechariah's *Benedictus*, and Simeon's *Nunc Dimittis* (which means, literally, "Now thou lettest depart . . .").

The angels rejoiced and sang because the incarnation reveals God's glory, His love, His holiness. Paul would later write, "Great is the mystery of godliness: God was manifest in the flesh" (1 Tim. 3:16 KJV). A mysterious, beautiful Savior, He is.

The hymn writer Charles Wesley beckoned us to listen to the song of the angels on Christmas. To "hark" is to hear, to bend the ear. What are these heralds, these messengers saying?

To us, twenty-one centuries later, it's a word that this broken, seemingly intractable world is not all there is. On that night

If you expect Christ, He will come. If you disbelieve, you will not hear the angels sing.

in Bethlehem, few heard the chorus, but some did—those, like the shepherds, whose hearts were soft, tuned to the Almighty. Mary and Joseph, Zechariah and Elizabeth, the magi, and those waiting in anticipation like Simeon and Anna. If you expect Christ, if you seek Him, He will come. If you disbelieve, like the scribes and religious leaders, you will not hear the angels sing.

This is not a generic "belief" as in the holiday classics that urge us to "just believe" in some nebulous Christmas spirit. This is to allow the Spirit to open our eyes to what is unseen, like Elijah's servant who suddenly saw the heavenly realm.

To believe is to read the Scripture and hear the distant sound of angel voices. To believe is to fall on our knees in adoration. It is to follow the Creator who first gave us life.

✦ One Glorious Day ✦

The angels said, "Peace on earth, good will toward men." But the original language really tells us it is about peace on earth toward *men of good will.* In other words, those who experience peace are those who have had their hearts cleansed by the sacrifice this Christ child was to bring.

The peace Jesus brought wasn't first world peace or some ethereal notion of unity. He brought peace between God and man. Peace toward those who accept the sacrifice of this final Passover Lamb.

Angels can only watch this special relationship between God and His people. God loves us with a love only experienced by humans. Angels cannot ever know His love like we do. Peter writes that they "long to look into" (1 Peter 1:12 NIV) the experience of redemption. They cannot love God and be loved by God like we can.

Kent Hughes reminds us:

> How we all would like to have been there—to be a fly on the ear of one of the shepherds' sheep. But actually, though the choir in Heaven played a major role, we on earth have the best part because we are the ones who receive God's grace. God became a man, not an angel. God redeemed us, not angels. Ours is the best part, and we will praise God for it for all eternity.[1]

Angels cannot receive grace, and yet they witness and behold the great love God has for you and for me. Dear Christian, as you read this, as you go through your Advent routines, do not miss this: Do you realize how much God loves you? So much that Jesus came and humbled Himself and became a baby. He endured all of the trappings of humanity. He dwelt among sinful, poor, wretched people. Why? Because of love.

The angels know how much God loves us, because they knew the whole plan, from creation to consummation. They see Christ pursuing His bride.

The angels have a perspective we don't share. Instead, God calls us to walk by faith, something that pleases God (Heb. 11:6). Angels can't exhibit faith; they can only see and behold God's glory when we live by faith. But by reveling in the Christmas story, by meditating this Advent, we can get a tiny glimpse of the heavenly vision.

In doing so, we begin to lift our eyes from the war and poverty and racism and disease and violence of this world and, like the angels, know that all of our days are being gathered by God as He gathers history to Himself.

And one glorious day, Jesus will come again as the conquering King. He will usher in perfect justice, and we will rule with Him as kings and queens of the universe. In this new city, the New Jerusalem, we'll be led in worship by the angels, joining in perfect harmony:

> *And the four living creatures, each of them with six wings, are full of eyes all around and within, and day and night they never cease to say,*
>
> *"Holy, holy, holy, is the Lord God Almighty,*
> *who was and is and is to come!"*
>
> *(Rev. 4:8)*

STUDY REFLECTION:

1. *Meditate on the angels' journey from Eden to Bethlehem to the New Jerusalem as described in the first part of this chapter.* Contemplate the way the story of Jesus runs through the Bible and through history.

2. *Read through the narratives in Luke 1 and 2 and in Matthew 1 and 2.*
   a. Write down specific characteristics of the angels.
   b. What were their messages to Mary, to Joseph, to the shepherds, and to the magi?

3. *Compare and contrast the experience of angels and the experience of humans in God's creation.*

4. *Write down three ways we are tempted, this Christmas, to be distracted from "hearing the voice of the angels" and worshiping the Christ child.*

5. *What are your own views on angels and their possible activity in the world today?*

SUGGESTED CHRISTMAS SONGS:

"O Holy Night"

"Hark! The Herald Angels Sing"

"Angels We Have Heard on High"

CHAPTER FIVE

Room for Jesus: The Innkeeper

Luke 2:7

*And she gave birth to her firstborn son and wrapped him
in swaddling cloths and laid him in a manger,
because there was no place for them in the inn.*

LUKE 2:7

For some reason, someone thought it was a good idea to forsake our warm beds and sleep "under the stars." I like the stars. I like the outdoors. But I wonder why, in the modern era with indoor plumbing, heat and air conditioning, and warm, modern beds, we still choose to sleep outside, in the elements, on purpose.

But alas, I was fifteen and it was the annual rite of passage for our Christian high school. We were in beautiful, unspoiled northern Minnesota where, for one night during our two-week stay, the guys would drag their sleeping bags and pillows and sleep outside.

Foolishly, I assumed that a typical sleeping bag would be sufficient to keep me warm on an April night in Minnesota. Well, no. I lay down as close to the campfire as I possibly could without setting myself on fire. And still I spent an entire night shifting around, shivering uncontrollably, and checking my watch.

It was one of the worst nights of sleep I've ever had. But it may not have been *the* worst.

There was the time our traveling college music group stopped to perform at a church somewhere in Pennsylvania. As often happens in these situations, we didn't book hotels but took up the church's offer to have us stay in church members' homes. The valuable lesson I learned this night was that simply because someone is kind enough to offer their home isn't a good enough reason to stay in that home.

Then, of course, there are those nights I've been stirred out of my sleep by my kids and their assortment of complaints: nightmares, vomiting, and the ever-present "leg pain." If I were to be honest, most of the time my wife has been the first one up while I pretend I'm in some kind of REM coma so I don't have to leave the warm sheets.

I imagine, though, that none of my fitful nights of sleep and none of yours were as difficult as the one endured by Mary and Joseph as they stumbled into Bethlehem, weary, hungry, and in need of a place to deliver a baby.

I don't know how you feel at the end of a long trip, but I usually just want everyone to get settled so I can crash into bed. And this is after a trip in a deluxe minivan with climate control, DVD players, and a cooler stocked with my favorite snacks.

Mary and Joseph made this journey in a world without automobiles, without truck stops, and without all the other modern conveniences that make our journeys at least bearable.

So imagine how Joseph felt after knocking on the door of the inn and asking, expectantly, "Do you have room for my pregnant wife and me?" You don't have to be a Greek scholar to understand the frustration he must have felt at the words that came back at him:

"No room in the inn."

There is not a ton of detail here. Scholars have debated throughout the centuries exactly what this means. What kind of inn was this? Many believe the roadside dwellings in those days were little more than a collection of modest shacks, surrounding an inner circle where animals and other livestock were kept. Others speculate that this was nothing more than a cave with some livable space carved out. What we do know and what we can be certain of is this: the accommodations were not five-star.

I'm guessing this couple, in this moment, wasn't exactly feeling Christmas cheer. Joseph probably wasn't meditating on the angel's words of encouragement to him when he first learned his wife was pregnant with the Son of God. And Mary was probably not, in between birth contractions, pondering the words of the innkeeper and treasuring them in her heart.

Like any normal couple with unexpected travel woes, they likely grew frustrated. Joseph racking his brain for what to do. Mary, ready to go into labor, hoping her husband-to-be will figure something out ASAP.

When Joseph and Mary said yes to God's plan, they likely didn't think this would mean enduring the grueling journey of the ninety miles from Nazareth to Bethlehem. And they were certainly not expecting there to be no room to physically give birth to the promised Messiah, the Christ child, the King of the universe. But here they were.

✦ Who Is at My Door? ✦

So who exactly opened the door to the inn and gave Joseph and Mary the bad news? Who exactly is this innkeeper we've been angry at for two thousand years?

The Bible doesn't exactly give us much here. Luke doesn't describe a specific innkeeper, standing at the door of the Bethlehem Hilton with a wagging finger and a no-vacancy sign. Much of what we think about this mythical figure is in our sacred imagination.

And yet, though the Bible doesn't mention an innkeeper, we have to imagine that there was someone present who let Joseph and Mary know, to quote Luke, that there was no room at this inn.

One thing we can be sure of: this was no ordinary night in this humble village inn. Over the years many travelers passed by, stopped in, and spent a night or two. All have been forgotten. But on this sacred night, an otherwise ordinary-looking couple asked for a room. A couple that history would remember, who bore not just another Jewish baby, but the Son of God.

This is the night about which we have sung, written, and worshiped in the two thousand years since that fateful knock on the door. A night of humility and holiness, when the King of heaven entered time and space, put on human flesh, and submitted Himself to the humiliation of this crude birth. This was a night for the ages.

Some of our greatest literature comes from the scene Luke describes here in chapter 2. The church fathers, for instance, waxed poetic about the meaning of Jesus' birth. Jerome calls attention to the humility of Bethlehem:

The Lord is born on earth, and he does not have even a cell in which to be born, for there was no room for him in the inn. The entire human race had a place, and the Lord about to be born on earth had none. He found no room among men. He found no room in Plato, none in Aristotle, but in a manger, among beasts of burden and brute animals, and among the simple, too, and the innocent.[1]

John Chrysostom reminds us that Jesus' crude birth was to demonstrate His humanity:

To prevent you from thinking that his coming to earth was merely an accommodation, and to give you solid grounds for truly believing that his was real flesh, he was conceived, born and nurtured. That his birth might be made manifest and become common knowledge, he was laid in a manger, not in some small room but in a lodging place before numerous people. This was the reason for the swaddling clothes and also for the prophecies spoken long before. The prophecies showed not only that he was going to be a man but that he would be conceived, born and nurtured as any child would be.[2]

Our hymn writers have sharpened their quills and given us their most beautiful reflections. Think of the scene that is painted in our minds every Christmas when we sing out our favorite carols, such as "O Little Town of Bethlehem" and "Silent Night."

There is, to be sure, not much certainty about the exact circumstances of His birth. Scholars will continue to quibble. Was it an inn? A spare room in someone's home? A cave? A grotto? I've had the chance to visit the grotto underneath the Church of the Nativity in Bethlehem, the place where some think Jesus' birth actually happened. It was a small space, untouched by time, where pilgrims have traveled for most of church history. We don't know if this is the place, but we who stood there hoped it was, the spot of earth where the Son of God entered this world as a baby.

It is significant, I think, that the meticulous gospel writer Luke made sure we would read that there was "no room for him in the inn." This was a statement of fact. The God who made the world found "nowhere to lay his head" (Luke 9:58).

More than two thousand Christmases later, we still have not exhausted the majesty of this night. After forty years of attending Christmas services, of reading Luke 2, of singing the carols, my heart is freshly awakened and my sense of awe at the scene: the Son of God, the King of the world, the One who spoke creation and breathed humanity into existence, vulnerable and bloody, crying and needy, human and yet, mysteriously, divine.

✦   **The Infant Disrupter**   ✦

This mystery was not, of course, on the mind of the proprietor of this Bethlehem establishment. He wasn't reading the church fathers, and he was not humming "Silent Night." It was just another day. Caesar's census had sent people into his town.

Joseph, who lived in Nazareth, made the trek like many others to his ancestral hometown. Joseph, a son of David, brought Mary to give birth in the place where the prophet Micah had predicted centuries before:

> *But you, O Bethlehem Ephrathah,*
> *who are too little to be among the clans of Judah,*
> *from you shall come forth for me*
> *one who is to be ruler in Israel,*

whose coming forth is from of old,
  from ancient days.
(Mic. 5:2)

But as he was making his final rounds, closing up his establishment and beginning to settle in for the night, this innkeeper likely didn't have Micah in his head. The couple who suddenly showed up at his door was a disruption, an inconvenience, a problem he didn't plan for.

This is, by the way, how God often enters our lives.

✦ A shepherd boy was busy tending sheep when he was summoned inside and a priest named Samuel poured oil on his head and whispered in his ear that he'd be Israel's next king (1 Sam. 16:1–13).

✦ A pagan farmer was minding his herds when God called him to leave everything and take his wife to a land called Canaan (Gen. 12).

✦ A fallen prince was working the backside of the desert when God appeared in a flaming bush and told him to go to Egypt (Ex. 3).

✦ A high-ranking member of the Sanhedrin was on his way to Damascus, putting down this new religious cult, when Jesus met him in a blinding light on the way to Damascus (Acts 9).

Few in Bethlehem were ready, anticipating the Son of God to show up on their doorsteps, certainly not this Hebrew business owner. This was just another couple trying to find space in a crowded Bethlehem.

What the innkeeper didn't know was that this night was no accident. Caesar's calling of the census. Joseph and Mary's decision to trek back to their ancestral hometown. Even the crowded nature of his inn. None of these events were coincidental. They were all part of God's divine plan to save the world.

Caesar didn't know that his census calling would be used by God to raise up a true and better ruler. The innkeeper didn't know that the cattle trough he dusted off and used to find room for Mary's baby would hold the head of the Son of God. The other travelers that day, who just happened to stay at this establishment, didn't know they'd be sleeping next to the promised Messiah.

We can't know how this impacted the innkeeper and his family and everyone who was there that sacred night. What did they think, for instance, when the shepherds poured into this tiny inn and offered worship of the just-born baby? Did they join in? Did they stare in wonder? Did they leave the next day scratching their heads at the experience?

We are tempted, with the hindsight of twenty centuries, to judge. Could the innkeeper not have found better accommodations for Jesus? Could he not have given up his own bed for a pregnant woman? But before we judge, we should examine our own hearts this Christmas. We, too, are often disrupted by Jesus.

We are religious up until the point it costs us something. We want a Jesus who forms Himself around our priorities and who can be sprinkled on top of our agendas. But Jesus invades our lives and disrupts them.

He asks us to leave our nets and follow Him. He asks us to drop our ambitions and join His mission. He asks us to leave behind our idols and worship Him with devotion.

While we were yet sinners, while we were apathetic, ignorant, and unfazed, Jesus came for us. This is the Jesus who knocks. Frederick Buechner, in his book *The Hungering Dark*, writes:

> Those who believe in God can never in a way be sure of Him again. Once they have seen Him in a stable, they can never be sure where He will appear or to what lengths He will go or to what ludicrous depths of self-humiliation He will descend in His wild pursuit of man . . . . there is no place or time so lowly and earthbound but that holiness can be present there too.[3]

Where we least expect Him, He comes most fully. He invades our lives; He goes where there is no room so we might find a home in Him. The One who had no home is making a home for us (John 14:3). The One who had no place to lay His head is our rest, our comfort, our joy.

In the end, the innkeeper—whoever he or she was—found room for Jesus. This Christmas I pray the same can be said about you and me.

STUDY REFLECTIONS:

1. *Reread Luke 2:*
   a. *What strikes you about the humility of Jesus' birth?*
   b. *Try to imagine the innkeeper's disposition and Joseph and Mary's response.*
   c. *Imagine the scene, the birth, and the way it affected those who were fellow travelers in this inn in Bethlehem.*

2. *Reflect on the holiness of this night:*
   a. *The Son of God was born in the most crude of circumstances.*
   b. *Why did God choose this setting and scene for the entrance of Jesus into the world?*
   c. *What does this tell us about the nature of the kingdom of God?*

3. *Meditate on these powerful quotes by some early church fathers:*
   a. *"There is no room in the inn by the wayside because Jesus by his incarnation now becomes our way home" (Bede).*[4]
   b. *"He was a baby and a child, so that you may be a perfect human. He was wrapped in swaddling clothes, so that you may be freed from the snares of death. He was in a manger, so that you may be in the altar. He was on earth that you may be in the stars. He had no other place in the inn, so that you may have many mansions in the heavens" (Ambrose).*[5]

CHAPTER SIX

The First to Know: Shepherds

Luke 2:1-21

*And in the same region there were shepherds out in the field,
keeping watch over their flock by night. And an angel of the Lord
appeared to them, and the glory of the Lord shone around them,
and they were filled with great fear. And the angel said to them,
"Fear not, for behold, I bring you good news of great joy that will
be for all the people. For unto you is born this day in the city
of David a Savior, who is Christ the Lord. And this will be a sign
for you: you will find a baby wrapped in swaddling cloths
and lying in a manger."*

LUKE 2:8–12

I n the last months of the year, many media outlets will publish
year-end retrospectives. I always enjoy watching these or flipping
through a national magazine that lists the top stories of the year. I love
reading about stories I had long since forgotten and remembering all
the celebrities who passed away. Sometimes we even do this with our
own personal lives, creating photo books out of momentous family
events.

Well, on one cool night in Bethlehem, a story was unfolding that would not only be the most significant event in that year for those who lived in Israel, it would be the most significant event in the history of the world. That's not hyperbole. This was the story the Jewish people eagerly awaited: the fulfillment of the promise delivered by the prophets and passed down from generation to generation.

God had issued an unconditional promise to the people of Israel. Out of their nation, out of the tribe of Judah, out of the family of their beloved King David, would come a Messiah. Then, after four hundred years of seeming silence, God spoke through an angel and informed a Jewish couple that the Christ child would be born into their family. Mary, a virgin, would conceive of the Holy Spirit and bear Jesus.

So you would think that when this story finally broke, when the baby Jesus finally broke free of Mary's womb and entered the world, that the announcement would be rolled out, by the Almighty, with the greatest fanfare. At least this is what I would do.

I'd leak it to a prominent journalist. I'd make sure those in the highest levels of authority were briefed. And I'd schedule a press conference. The cable shows would cover it. It would be trending on social media.

But this wasn't the way Jesus Christ, the Son of God, the second person of the Trinity, made His appearance.

✦ A Most Humble Entrance ✦

During this time, a lot was happening on the world stage. The great-nephew of Julius Caesar, Octavian, had just been crowned the new Caesar. We know Octavian by the name "Augustus," given to him by the Roman Senate as a way to confer godlike status.[1]

Augustus was one of the first Roman monarchs to demand worship, and his people were not hesitant to offer it. After all, this was the ruler who had achieved peace.

To most of the world, Caesar was god, life would forever be Roman, and for the Jewish people, the dream of a Messiah King was all but dead, except to the minority who actually read and studied and believed the ancient prophets.

Luke's narrative begins with a call by Caesar for a census and a tax. Little did this now-forgotten ruler understand that his demand for a census was used by God to set in motion events that would ultimately lead to the birth of a King who, unlike Caesar, would have a throne that would never end. Caesar's declaration forced a common village carpenter and his pregnant, teenage bride to make the journey from Nazareth to Bethlehem, a journey that undoubtedly taxed the strength of this young woman.

What Caesar didn't know was that the baby in the womb of this peasant woman was the very Messiah the Jewish people had longed for, the One whose birth would change the world forever.

The most significant life in the history of the world was in Mary's womb.

This baby inside Mary was not a Caesar, who fashioned himself as a god, but He was the very God of the universe, God in the flesh. I love what the late pastor J. Vernon McGee had to say about the events of that night in Bethlehem:

> Everything that happened was arranged by God. If anyone had said
> to Caesar, "Wait a minute; women about to give birth are going to

have to be moved in order for you to get your taxes," I think he would have replied, "I do not care about babies or their mothers; I am only interested in taxes, armies, money and luxury." Well, that is all gone now, including Caesar.²

✦ Where's the Celebration? ✦

But when you think about what was happening that night, when the mystery of God coming down to dwell among His people, the mystery of Jesus being born as fully man and yet fully God, the long-awaited promised One finally broke free, where was the celebration?

In a small town, with poverty-stricken parents, born in a smelly grotto, was the Son of God.

Caesar should have been there to worship Jesus, but he wasn't.

Herod should have been there to worship Jesus, but he wasn't.

The people of Israel should have been there to worship Jesus, but they weren't.

The nations of the world should have bowed down to this baby, but they didn't.

Later the apostle John would say that Jesus visited His own—and His own did not receive Him (John 1:11).

This wasn't a big deal among most of the world, but it was a big deal in heaven. It was a big deal among the people of God, the true believers who anticipated Christ's coming. Christmas is a powerful reminder that what is important in heaven is often unimportant on earth.

While the world was sleeping, the Son of God made His entrance. And this was cause for celebration in heaven as the host of heaven rejoiced at the unfolding of God's plan. For four hundred years, God had been silent. There were no prophets, no angels appearing, nothing miraculous. But now the heavens opened with rejoicing. And the news came to the people you'd least expect to employ as your messengers of this good news.

✦ Why Shepherds? ✦

A couple of years ago, I had the opportunity to appear on a top-rated national morning show. When I got the email confirming my appearance, my stomach tightened a bit and I think my feet lifted off the ground. My first thought was, *Wow, this will sell a ton of books.* And my second thought was, *Do I need to buy a new suit?* I was excited and yet very, very nervous. Somehow I managed to get through the experience without totally embarrassing myself.

Betting on a big-time television news show is one of the best ways to try to announce big news. Public relations professionals work hard at securing these opportunities, trying to get their guests in front of millions of eyeballs. But when God announced the birth of Jesus to the world, He used the opposite approach. He didn't send Jesus to 30 Rock but sent the host of heaven to a common field outside Bethlehem. And the people He chose as His spokesmen were unpolished, sweaty, uncouth shepherds.

Today shepherds are romanticized in every single Christmas pageant. Many of us have donned a modified pillowcase and grabbed a walking stick and appeared in a Christmas pageant at church or school. But in the first century, nobody thought shepherds were cute. And certainly nobody thought they were important. But there they were, the first to know at Christmas.

Shepherds were not really considered part of polite society in those days. They were required to tend their flocks outside the city gates. The only reason shepherds had any significance was because sheep were a valuable commodity, especially as it got closer to Passover, when many lambs would be sacrificed in the temple.

The work of a shepherd was (and still is) extraordinarily difficult. They had to wrangle obstinate sheep. They had to ensure their flocks were well fed. And they had to fend off predators: wolves or even larger animals like bears or lions. Sometimes unsavory characters would come in and try to steal the sheep. This is why shepherds were awake on this night. Most likely they were sleeping in shifts, ensuring the livestock was not compromised.

And yet there is something significant and powerful about the inclusion of the shepherds in the Jesus story. Luke is reminding us, by mentioning the shepherds, that the kingdom of God isn't just for the insiders, but for outsiders, like shepherds, like the poor classes Mary and Joseph came from. It reminds us that the kingdom of God is often made up, not of the noble and wise, but of the underclass, those people that have no business being near royalty. Immanuel, God with us, means God is truly among all classes of people, not simply the connected or well-resourced.

The presence of the shepherds in the Christmas story also tells us a little bit about just what kind of Messiah Jesus would be. He would come to us as a Savior, as a King, as a Lion, but also as our Shepherd. Though their vocation was not viewed with respect by their peers, Scripture always portrays shepherding as a high calling, perhaps the most repeated image of leadership in the Bible.

God refers to Himself as Israel's Shepherd (Gen. 48:15; 49:24; Jer. 31:10). In David's famous psalm, he is grateful that "the LORD is my shepherd" (Ps. 23). And the prophets Ezekiel (22) and Jeremiah (10; 23; 50) often warned God's people about poor shepherds—bad leaders who exploit rather than lead. To shepherd, in God's world, is to sacrificially care for those vulnerable in your care. Shepherds in those days didn't drive their herds but gently led them.

Today, even in some Christian circles, leadership as shepherding is viewed as negatively as it might have been among the sophisticated in the first century. Though spiritual leaders in Scripture, from Old to New Testament, are often compared to shepherds, some evangelical leadership texts dismiss this idea. I once heard a prominent pastor mock the idea, saying that a CEO or a general is a better description of Christian leadership. But it's hard to dismiss how intentional the Holy Spirit is in including this vision of gentle yet firm leadership both as the way God leads His people and how God intends those who follow them to lead. Jesus' last words to Peter were "Feed my sheep" (John 21). This is how we demonstrate God's love, by taking care of others with soft hands and compassion.

This is why I believe the announcement of the coming of Jesus—who called Himself the Good Shepherd (John 10:11)—had to happen in a shepherds' field among those who lead sheep. Luke is telling us that this ruler who is to come would be different than the rulers His people were used to seeing. He wouldn't be a Caesar who ruled only by brute force. He wouldn't be a Herod, who governed by treachery, murder, and paranoia. No, Jesus, would be, among all of His attributes, a shepherd. And He would entrust Himself and His message to shepherds.

The Lamb of God would first be held and handled and touched by those who knew how to appreciate and care for a lamb. And yet more than anybody, these shepherds knew the ultimate fate of each lamb for which they cared. I imagine they heard the prophecy of Isaiah more keenly than anyone in Israel. They tended the very lambs that would be sacrificed at Passover. And yet a Lamb had come who would be the final sacrifice. This Lamb wouldn't simply cover their sins as the sacrifices did, but He'd actually become sin. John the Baptist said about Jesus later, "Behold, the Lamb of God, who takes away the sin of the world!"

The good news of the coming of the Lamb of God, slain for the sins of the world, announced among lambs set aside for the temple sacrifice and in the city of David, Israel's last great shepherd. This is God declaring to His people that Jesus, both the Good Shepherd and the Lamb of God, was coming to make true peace between God and man.

✦ Belief and Awe ✦

One minute they were watching the flocks, maybe catching a few minutes of sleep after a night shift, and the next minute they were witnesses to salvation history. The display in the heavens must have been spectacular, as the sky around them filled with the host of heaven praising God and worshiping Him. I have no doubt that this wasn't just a small ensemble of angels or the chief angels but the host of heaven. Not even the greatest performance on earth with the most talented musicians could parallel the incredible celebration that unfolded on the big screen of the sky before these shepherds. The plan of God, conceived from time immemorial, the plan of redemption, promised

It's not like the shepherds got an email invite the day before: *Meet up at field 1 for an epic event!*

in the garden, was unfolding before their eyes.

I always find it interesting how God seems, throughout Scripture, to interrupt and show up in the middle of an ordinary person's daily routine. It's not like the shepherds got an email invite the day before: *Meet up at field 1 for an epic event!* And yet even though they were caught by surprise, these men of humble means and reputation responded in ways that prove God's wisdom in entrusting the announcement of the birth of Jesus to them.

They believed.

These men saw the angels, heard the witness, and believed. The scribes were too jaded. The royals were too sophisticated. The Romans were too dismissive. But these humble outsiders had the simple faith to look up, listen, and put their faith in the Christ child.

They could be awed.

The world of the first century was pretty cynical. False messiahs had come and gone. The promise of Israel's restoration seemed more like a pipe dream. And the Roman flag waved high above the temple mount. And yet here were people still willing to be awed. Luke says the shepherds possessed great fear. And wouldn't you? You're a lowly shepherd in a backwater town in a ravaged land *and all of a sudden the heavens open and angels start singing!* Yes, you'd be fearful.

And yet there is something wonderful about the ability to still be awed by God. Today's world is just as jaded as the world of the first century. Smart people are way too enlightened to believe in the supernatural. And yet Proverbs says that "the fear of the LORD is the beginning of wisdom" (9:10). Real spirituality is a healthy awe, reverence, and fear of God, to know that you're nothing and God is awesome.

The closer you are to heaven, the greater your fear and awe of God. Not fear in a sense of being scared, but being awed.

I hope that this Christmas season your heart is open to awe and wonder. It's easy to treat our religious traditions, especially Christmas, as a sort of ho-hum affair. But God visits those who are willing to fear and to awe, to wonder and to meditate. Have we stopped what we are doing long enough to see what God is doing around us? Have we sufficiently unplugged from the digital distractions that keep our minds moving but distract us from the supernatural? Are you willing to be awed by an awesome and powerful God and by the mystery of the incarnation of Jesus Christ?

Fearsome? Yes. But there is a sense in which our fear turns to faith. The angels said, "Fear not." Why? Because Jesus is a Shepherd we should fear, but no longer have to be afraid of. This royal announcement on a cold night in Bethlehem meant that those who put their faith in this baby Jesus would experience peace with God. This is what the angels meant by "on earth peace among those with whom he is pleased." In one sense, the angels were reminding the shepherds that the temporary peace currently being experienced in the Roman Empire would one day give way to war. But only this Prince of Peace could usher in genuine *shalom,* true renewal. And this baby Jesus would offer *personal* peace with God. The One who came to shepherds would be the Good Shepherd of their souls. The Lamb of God would fully atone for sin. No more would worshipers need to sacrifice actual lambs.

They lived with purpose.

Luke makes sure we know that the shepherds didn't waste time gazing into the Bethlehem sky. Once they heard the witness of the angels they "came with haste," to quote the King James Version. And wouldn't you? They couldn't keep this message to themselves. They abandoned all pretenses and bolted into Bethlehem, sheep and all, to find the Messiah. Imagine the sight they must have been, knocking on doors, awaking the locals, shouting the good news that the long-awaited Messiah had finally come. They didn't simply marvel at the message. They believed it, and it changed their direction. A temptation for us, this Christmas, is to simply get full of "the feels," the warm sentimentality of this season, and miss the good news at the heart of the holiday: Christ has come into the world to save you and to save me. The angel told the shepherds that this good news was "for all people." It was personal.

I like what one commentator says: "The truth is, even if Christ were born in Bethlehem a thousand times but not within you, you would be eternally lost. The Christ who was born into the world must be born in your heart. Religious sentiment, even at Christmastime, without the living Christ is a yellow brick road to darkness."[3]

They left their fields and became the most unlikely of messengers, these roughly hewn, untrained, likely illiterate shepherd boys. John Calvin says of them, "Though God had, at his command, many honorable and distinguished witnesses, he passed by them, and chose shepherds, person of humble rank, and of no account among men."[4] They became the world's first missionaries, the first in a long line of ordinary, unheralded messengers of the gospel. God is on the move, building His church around the world, mostly through people you will never hear of: folks without significant Twitter followings, with no official titles, and of whom the world is not worthy.

Go tell it on the mountain, the Christmas hymn urges us, that Jesus Christ is born!

STUDY REFLECTIONS:

1. *Consider the significance of shepherds in the Bible.*

   a. *Look up Genesis 48:15, 49:24, Jeremiah 31:10, Psalm 23, and John 10 and meditate on the way God refers to Himself as a Shepherd of His people.*

   b. *Look up Ezekiel 34 and compare it with Acts 20:25–31 and 1 Peter 5:2.*

2. *Read together, as a family, Luke 2:1–21.*

   a. *Consider how the shepherds reacted to the message of the angels:*
   - ✦ *They believed.*
   - ✦ *They worshiped.*
   - ✦ *They went to tell others.*

3. *Questions to ask yourself this Christmas:*

   a. *Have I paused to wonder in awe at the miracle of the incarnation?*

   b. *With whom am I going to share the story of Christmas? How can I "believe, worship, and tell the story"?*

SUGGESTED CHRISTMAS SONG:

"Immanuel" by Melanie Penn

MEDITATE ON THIS QUOTE . . .

Who, then, are those to whom this joyful news is to be proclaimed?
Those who are faint-hearted and feel the burden of their sins, like
the shepherds, to whom the angels proclaim the message, letting the
great lords in Jerusalem, who do not accept it, go on sleeping.[5]

– Martin Luther

Seeking and Finding:
The Wise Men

Matthew 2:1–12

Now after Jesus was born in Bethlehem of Judea in the days
of Herod the king, behold, wise men from the east came to
Jerusalem, saying, "Where is he who has been born
king of the Jews? For we saw his star when it rose
and have come to worship him."

MATTHEW 2:1-2

When you grow up in the church like I did, one of the enduring symbols of Christmas is the wise men and their camels. Every year, the church I grew up in held massive, community-wide, multi-day Christmas pageants. This was no ordinary church program. It was an elaborate affair, complete with live animals, original music scores, and, yes, church members dressed up in satin gowns as wise men.

In fact, to this day, when I hear the music to "Joyful, Joyful, We Adore Thee," I can picture Dave, a longtime church staff member, atop a camel making his entrance into the auditorium.

The wise men are a regular feature at Christmas. They adorn our nativity sets. They appear on our Christmas cards. And regular church folk named Dave get to don satin gowns and ride camels. But what's funny about the wise men is how little we actually know about them. Or, more accurately, how much we get wrong about these mysterious monarchs.

✦ So Who Are the Wise Men? ✦

Don't worry. I'm not going to be that guy who spoils every Christmas by pointing out the historical inaccuracies of our cherished yuletide beliefs. Every gathering has a Scrooge like this, who either just graduated from seminary or is busy writing a blog post telling us that the first Christmas probably wasn't in the winter.

But I think it is important to know more about these traveling sages. There has been a lot of speculation throughout church history, mainly because the Bible is somewhat vague on the details.

We get the word "wise men" in our English translations as a way of interpreting the word *magos*, which typically means something like "those who have wisdom through investigation and interpretation of the movements of heavenly bodies."[1] Matthew tells us they came "from the East." Many have speculated that perhaps they came from Persia, now modern-day Iraq. This would seem to make sense, though we cannot be sure about it. Many in the East were watchers of the stars, often divining special meaning and purpose.

Could it be that they were from Babylon, where Jewish exiles were taken? The book of Daniel records the use of "wise men" (Dan. 2:2, 10 NET) to help the kings understand their dreams and visions. It's not hard to imagine that someone like Daniel, who rose to prominent positions in Babylon and was outspoken about his faith in the coming

Messiah, had an influence on several generations of Eastern intellectuals.

It's likely there were more than three wise men, given how much of a stir they caused when they arrived in Jerusalem.

Were there three of them? And were they kings, as the famous hymn, "We Three Kings," seems to indicate? Probably not. We get the idea of three from the three gifts offered, but it's likely that the gifts were presented as a whole by the entire delegation. And it's likely there were more than three, given how much of a stir Matthew says they caused when they arrived in Jerusalem. One early church father speculated that perhaps there were fourteen (!) wise men. I don't know about that, but this was probably a caravan of quite a few people. They weren't kings, but they were prominent and influential religious leaders from the East.

What is clear to us is that the magi were earnest in their desire to find the King of the Jews. They combined their knowledge of the Old Testament Scriptures with a reliance on astrology. Scripture speaks pretty strongly against looking to the stars for meaning, but here is God meeting these seekers where they are, utilizing His power over the heavenly bodies to direct them to His Son.

This doesn't mean the Bible condones astrology, but it does show us that God is willing to meet those who genuinely seek Him. Consider how God met us. My guess is very few of us were completely sound in our theology when we first met Jesus. And yet God can meet a seeking sinner, with impure motives and uncertain beliefs, and point that soul to His Son.

And consider what tools God employed here in this story to let the world know about the birth of His Son, Jesus. The entire universe was at God's disposal in announcing the gospel. In Luke we read of the angelic messengers and the way the sky lit up with praise as the heavenly choir shouted the news to the shepherds. And in Matthew, we read of God using a star to point people from afar toward Bethlehem.

This story has a connection to the Old Testament. There is an obscure story in the book of Numbers (22–24) of an irascible prophet named Balaam and a talking donkey. God asked Balaam to deliver three blessings to his people. One of those, the final message, contained these words:

> *"the oracle of him who hears the words of God,*
> *and knows the knowledge of the Most High,*
> *who sees the vision of the Almighty,*
> *falling down with his eyes uncovered:*
> *I see him, but not now;*
> *I behold him, but not near:*
> *a star shall come out of Jacob,*
> *and a scepter shall rise out of Israel;*
> *it shall crush the forehead of Moab*
> *and break down all the sons of Sheth."*
> *(Num. 24:16–17)*

Some have speculated that perhaps this was just a coincidence, perhaps a comet that might have been in the sky at the same time. And perhaps a comet did lead the wise men to Bethlehem, but there is no doubt here that this was the God who appeared as a pillar of fire and a cloud to His people, opening up the heavens to point the lost to Jesus.

All of creation is at God's disposal to tell His story. King David, describing the joy that would one day cause the universe to announce the son of David born in the city of David, says:

The heavens declare the glory of God,
and the sky above proclaims his handiwork.
Day to day pours out speech,
and night to night reveals knowledge.
There is no speech, nor are there words,
whose voice is not heard.
Their voice goes out through all the earth,
and their words to the end of the world.
In them he has set a tent for the sun,
which comes out like a bridegroom leaving his chamber,
and, like a strong man, runs its course with joy.
(Ps. 19:1–5)

The nineteenth-century British pastor Charles Spurgeon said this about the star that led these men to Jesus:

He was born of lowly parents, laid in a manger, and wrapped in infant clothes. But the principalities and powers in the heavenly places are in motion. First, an angel descends to proclaim the advent of the newborn king. But the activity was not confined to the spirits above, for in the heavens above the earth something began to stir. A star is sent on behalf of all the stars, as if it were the envoy of all worlds to represent them before their king. This star was put into commission to await the Lord, to be his herald to men far away, and to be God's usher to conduct these wise men into Christ's presence.[2]

It gives me goose bumps to think of this moment, when the star first appeared to those seeking sages in the East. The infant Son of

God, Creator of the heavens and earth, who holds the universe in His hands, directing the stars to draw people to Himself. This shows us the love of God for the world. God so loved the world, Jesus would later say (John 3:16), that God offered His Son for the redemption of those who believe.

Perhaps this is a dreary winter day for you, when you are not feeling all the Christmas feels. Maybe you are lonely and discouraged. Perhaps you've been rejected. But know this: if you are in Christ, God leveraged the entire universe to shout to you His message of love and drew you to Himself.

✦ The Two Kings ✦

So we don't believe these wise men were really kings (though singing the hymn is still okay—it's one of my favorites), but there *are* kings in this passage and this, I believe, is the point of Matthew including this story in his retelling of the birth of Jesus.

If Luke emphasizes Jesus as a servant, Matthew's gospel is all about Jesus as King. This is why he opens with a genealogy (more on that in another chapter), establishing Jesus as rightful heir to the throne of David. And it's why here Matthew sets up a contrast with another king, Herod, the bloodthirsty ruler of the Jews appointed by Rome. This is Herod the Great, who kept power by attacking and often killing his political enemies (and even family members) and who built impressive architecture in Israel.

The prominent and wealthy men from the East traveled far and wide, not to sit at the feet of the one who sat on a throne in Jerusalem, but to bow before an infant in a house in Bethlehem. The star from heaven didn't point to Herod, but to Jesus.

Matthew is telling us that true worshipers worship the true King. While most of Israel slept in spiritual lethargy and those who knew the Scriptures—the scribes and the chief priests—were more fearful of Herod than God, these men had the faith to worship the One who deserved worship: Jesus.

The presence of these men from the East—outsiders, Gentiles—is a confirmation of God's promise to send a Messiah who would not only be the King of the Jews, but a Messiah for the nations. Jesus' kingdom is a kingdom not just for insiders, but for outsiders. In fact, many insiders—those who were closest to Jesus—were most resistant to His message. And so it often is today. Those who are most "churched" are often those who are so blinded by self-righteousness they cannot see—we cannot see—the gospel. And it is often those who seem so far from God whom God by His Spirit is drawing.

This should also give us pause when we begin to think that the gospel is only for people who look like us, who come from our backgrounds, who speak our language. The truth is that if you live in the West, you are likely one of the "outsiders" to whom the gospel had to be extended; you are part of the Gentile nations who were furthest from Jesus. We should thank

> **Let's pray that our churches begin to reflect heaven's reality: the beautiful diversity of the kingdom of God.**

God that His promise wasn't only for a certain ethnic group, but that in His kingdom, we see every nation, tribe, and tongue represented (Rev. 7). This is a global kingdom. Let's pray that our churches begin to reflect heaven's reality: the beautiful diversity of the kingdom of God.

✦ Bowing Before the Real King ✦

The name "wise men" is the term that has most stuck to these mysterious magi from the East, and perhaps it's just as well. For their wisdom was not in their own intellect or their knowledge of the stars, but in their willingness to know where the true source of wisdom is.

It wasn't, they knew, in their own Eastern religions. It wasn't, they discovered, in Jerusalem where they thought the King of the Jews should be. It wasn't even amongst the religious leaders who should have joined them in their quest to find Jesus.

True wisdom is found, they realized, at the feet of Jesus.

Imagine this scene here in Bethlehem. The text tells us that after a fruitless inquiry in Herod's temple, the star that had risen in the East suddenly appeared again, leading them to the exact house where Mary and Joseph and the now-infant Jesus lived. Jesus was, contrary to our nativity scenes and Christmas pageants, not a baby when the magi showed up and no longer in the cradle. Judging by Herod's murderous edict, we can assume Jesus is about two years old. But even though they missed the birth, it doesn't make this long journey of worship any less significant.

They had scanned the skies and pored through the ancient texts. They had plodded through deserts and made their way over mountains. They had knocked on doors and tiptoed into temples. These men and their entourage rode and walked and climbed their way from their home to a place so completely foreign to them. And yet the journey of the wise men pales in comparison to the One they now venerated. Jesus had the longer trip, leaving the throne of heaven and coming to live amongst His people.

This is why the magi's response was one of worship and exaltation of the Christ child. Let's stop and meditate on this moment here. These were men of the world, wise and cultured and sophisticated in every way. They came expecting a young king on a throne, surrounded by servants and the trappings of royalty. What they found, instead, was a poor family in an otherwise quiet neighborhood. To the average onlooker, unfamiliar with the ancient prophecies and unaware of the guiding star, this was all so pedestrian.

But to those whose hearts were open to God's leading, who were truly seeking Jesus, they saw what the prophets predicted, what the angels serenaded, and what Mary understood: there toddling in a dirty tunic was the Son of God. And so, these prestigious men dropped everything and offered the only right response to Jesus: worship.

The very sight is a bundle of contradictions: the young child receiving the worship of royalty. The wealthy bowing before the impoverished. And yet this is the upside-down nature of the kingdom of God.

In that moment, the real power was not in the wealthy coffers of these rich rulers. It was not in the gilded halls of Herod's palace. It was in the infant God-man standing before them. And so they bowed in reverent, real worship.

Jesus would later say that it is impossible for those of means to enter the kingdom of God (Matt. 19:24). This is because money and power—like that possessed by the wise men—can become idols that blind us to our own vulnerabilities and need for saving faith. But Jesus would also say that with God, all things are possible (Matt. 19:26). So here we have wealthy and connected and powerful people drawn by the Spirit of God into a humility that causes them to be brought low in worship of the Almighty. They had followed the star and now they worshiped the One who hung the stars.

In a sense, this a journey required not just of Eastern magi, but of anyone who is to enter the kingdom of God. God resists the proud, the Bible repeats over and over again, but dispenses His grace to the humble. Regardless of the size of your bank account, whether you grow up on the streets or Sunset Boulevard, to know Jesus is to bow and become low, to recognize your sinfulness and vulnerability, and to receive the grace of God. I love the words of Gregory the Great, who urges us to "like the magi, return to our home country [paradise] by another way than the way we left it."[3]

The Bible says that one day, everyone will be a worshiper, but for those who have resisted Jesus, it will be too late. Every knee will one day bow (Phil. 2:10), but the truly wise bow and worship while there is still time.

✦ A Costly Worship ✦

We should linger, this Christmas, on the depth of the worship exhibited by the magi. Matthew includes their story here as a way of letting us see how true worshipers worship the King.

Consider the fourfold response of the wise men:

They sought the truth by following the star and reading the ancient prophecies.

They obeyed the voice of the angel who told them to not return to Herod.

They bowed at the sight of Jesus.

They gave precious gifts as an act of devotion and worship.

Theirs was not a cheap worship. It was not a casual event. This was costly worship. I'm afraid our worship of Jesus, in a religiously saturated culture, is often flippant. We sing on Sundays without an excitement, and we too often approach the weekly gathering of saints with an inner eye roll. But if Jesus is the true King, if He is indeed the fulfillment of the covenant promises to Israel, if He is the Light of the world who saves people from their sins, then isn't He worthy of our whole selves, body and soul?

I just love the words of the fifth-century saint Chromatius, who observes this worshipful moment in Matthew and writes this:

> Let us now observe how glorious was the dignity that attended the King after his birth, after the magi in their journey remained obedient to the star. For immediately the magi fell to their knees and adored the one born as Lord. There in his very cradle they venerated him with offerings of gifts, though Jesus was merely a whimpering infant. They perceived one thing with the eyes of their bodies but another with the eyes of the mind. The lowliness of the body he assumed was discerned, but the glory of his divinity is now made manifest. A boy he is, but it is God who is adored.[4]

And today, our journey is not less important and our worship no less needed. Today God is calling true worshipers to gather and lift up our praise to the King of kings.

The wise men offered a costly worship. These men gave lavish, expensive gifts. There has been much speculation throughout church history as to the meaning of the gifts. We don't know exactly what they mean, but there are some ideas that can help provoke our own worship.

Gregory the Great suggested that the gold symbolized wisdom, the frankincense symbolized prayer offered toward God, and the myrrh an offering of our bodies as a living sacrifice (Rom. 12:1–2) a devotion of mind, soul, and body.[5]

More recently, some have suggested that perhaps the gold represents Jesus' kingship, the frankincense His deity (frankincense was often used as an offering to God), and the myrrh His humanity.[6] On that last gift, it is interesting to note that myrrh was offered to Jesus as a kind of painkiller as He agonized on the cross, and He refused it (Mark 15:23). It was also used as an embalming fluid at His burial (John 19:38–42). Is this a foreshadowing of the suffering and death Jesus would endure for sinners?

We can't be dogmatic about the meaning of the gifts, but we can be sure that true worship involves giving. Often in church life we are reticent to talk about things like tithing and giving. But giving is a natural overflow of a heart that is grateful for Jesus, who gave everything for us. Here nobody forced the magi to give. They did it willingly as the Spirit of God loosened their hands from their possessions. Giving doesn't get you to Jesus, but it is a sure sign that you've met Him.

This is one reason why Christians, while resisting the secularization of Christmas, can nevertheless be joyful gift-givers this time of year. We give gifts to each other and to the work of the Lord as a celebration. There is no reason to be cranky about opening presents and seeing the glow on our children's faces when they receive blessings from us. Our King has come, and His joy overflows from our hearts to our hands and into the lives of others.

STUDY REFLECTIONS:

1. **When you are confronted by Jesus this Christmas, which of these three responses best describes you:**

   a. **Adoration**—*The wise men, who sought Jesus at great personal sacrifice and would not give up until they could bow before Him in costly worship?*

   b. **Anger**—*Herod, who was threatened by the presence of Jesus, who disrupted Herod's quest for personal power and selfish ambition?*

   c. **Apathy**—*The scribes and priests, who knew the Scriptures and were in a place of worship (the temple) but who missed Jesus due to their fear of man and their self-righteousness and spiritual apathy?*

2. **Can you trace your own journey to Jesus?** *How did God work in the twists and turns of your life to bring you to His Son? Parents, this may be a wonderful opportunity to share with your children your own spiritual testimony.*

3. **How is worship of the Christ child this Christmas releasing generosity in your heart this year?** *As you make your shopping lists, are you giving out of duty, or delight that your King has come?*

SUGGESTED CHRISTMAS SONG:

"God with Us" by Todd Agnew

CHAPTER EIGHT

Herod, the Monster of Christmas

Matthew 2:1–23

Then Herod, when he saw that he had been tricked by the wise men, became furious, and he sent and killed all the male children in Bethlehem and in all that region who were two years old or under, according to the time that he had ascertained from the wise men. Then was fulfilled what was spoken by the prophet Jeremiah: "A voice was heard in Ramah, weeping and loud lamentation, Rachel weeping for her children; she refused to be comforted, because they are no more."

MATTHEW 2:16–18

Every year at this time, our family likes to gather around the TV and watch our favorite Christmas movies. In fact, one of my enduring traditions is to, sometime after Thanksgiving, program our DVR to record the Christmas movies as they are aired on television and to bookmark others on Netflix.

Perhaps our favorite story is Charles Dickens's *A Christmas Carol.* I've seen almost every movie version of it, from the old black-and-white productions to the creepy (but good) Jim Carrey version. I've attended numerous live productions and have even, as a young kid, performed in a weirdly sanitized church version.

A Christmas Carol is like most Christmas stories in that it features a villain, someone whose chief goal is to make Christmas miserable or nonexistent for everyone. Dickens gives us Scrooge (pre-transformation), but he's not unique. In fact, if you could find one theme in almost every holiday film it's that there is an antagonist:

✦ *It's a Wonderful Life* has Mr. Potter
✦ *The Grinch Who Stole Christmas* has, well, the Grinch
✦ *Home Alone* has Harry and Marv, the bumbling burglars

See what I mean? And every Hallmark Christmas movie has a guy trying to wreck Christmas. He's usually a heartless developer ready to bulldoze the family Christmas store/bakery/toy store who is only thwarted when the hunky barista comes to the rescue.

The original Christmas story has its own monster, though his cruelties are far from cute. Herod is a legitimate villain, which is why he's not usually included in many Christmas stories. I don't think any nativity sets include this guy.

But Herod figures very prominently in the Christmas story. To ignore him is to not only ignore the world into which Jesus was born, but to miss an important thread in God's grand plan of redemption. Underneath the warm glow of our Christmases is a dark thread of violence, signs of a cosmic war against all that is good.

✦ Back to the Garden ✦

To fully understand what is happening in Matthew's gospel, you have to leave the troubled streets of Jerusalem and the quiet town of Bethlehem and travel back thousands of years in history and hundreds of pages in your Bible.[1]

Because, as we have already seen, the characters in this story of Christmas are merely pawns in a larger spiritual battle. Paul writes in Ephesians:

> *For we do not wrestle against flesh and blood, but against the rulers, against the authorities, against the cosmic powers over this present darkness, against the spiritual forces of evil in the heavenly places.*
> *(6:12)*

At the heart of the incarnation, the story of God leaving heaven to become flesh, is the cosmic struggle between God and Satan. Ever since Lucifer, God's angel and the leader of the chorus of heaven, fell from glory (Isa. 14:12–14), he and his band of demons have had one singular mission: to thwart God's plans.

That's why the Christmas story doesn't really begin in 5 BC or in the gospel of Matthew, but centuries earlier, way back in a garden. Satan's first salvo comes in the opening pages of Scripture, not long after God created man and placed him in the beauty and perfection of Eden. Satan, inhabiting a snake, seduces the very first humans into rejecting their Father. Their disobedience stained the innocence into which they were created, injecting corruption into the cosmos and into every human heart (Rom. 5:12).

But Satan's attack didn't catch the Godhead by surprise. God would initiate a plan to rescue His image bearers and renew the world.

We see this in His words to Adam and Eve:

> *The LORD God said to the serpent, "Because you have done this,*
> *cursed are you above all livestock and above all beasts of the field; on*
> *your belly you shall go, and dust you shall eat all the days of your life.*
> *I will put enmity between you and the woman, and between your*
> *offspring and her offspring; he shall bruise your head, and you shall*
> *bruise his heel." (Gen. 3:14-15)*

Christmas, then, began long before that starry night in Bethlehem. It began in eternity, in the counsels of the Trinity, as God planned to redeem the world from sin. This would involve a long and bloody struggle between the offspring of Satan and the seed of the woman. We see this played out on the pages of the Old Testament, where, page after page, we find seemingly parallel tracks of good and evil:

+ A son of Adam, Cain slays his brother in cold blood, the seeming triumph of his works over Abel's righteous sacrifice. But God then raises up another generation in another of Adam's sons—Seth.
+ A son of Seth, Abraham, is called out of his homeland to follow the promise of God. But three times Abraham's family is threatened by famine, by sin, and by infertility. But God births a miracle in Isaac, the son of promise.
+ A son of Abraham, Jacob, endures family dysfunction, his own sinful scheming, and famine in the land. But God raises up his son Joseph to save Israel.
+ Four centuries later, an evil Pharaoh, who abandoned the way of Joseph, saw the immigrant people of God as a threat and determined, by exploitation and murder, to wipe out the chil-

dren of Abraham. But God raised up godly midwives to deliver babies from death and another son of Abraham, Moses, out of the bulrushes and out of the wilderness to be a deliverer.

✦ God led Samuel to anoint an obscure shepherd boy named David, who would slay Israel's enemies and whose throne would endure forever, but David would be forced to run from Saul and would often choose a path of sin and dysfunction.

✦ Throughout Israel's history, they would choose idols over worship of Yahweh, would be carried into captivity by other nations, and would be scattered around the world. And yet the prophets foretold of a time when a new King would arise who would be the final and true son of David.

✦ At one time, the house of David was threatened by a wicked Queen Athalia. But a godly couple hid the last remaining descendant, a baby named Joash, in a storage closet for six years.

✦ Satan recruited the wicked Haman, who threatened to use his power in Persia to eliminate God's people. But God empowered Esther and Mordecai to save His people.

Matthew is framing his book not as a tidy biography of Jesus but as the clash of kingdoms.

So now you know that when we read Matthew's account of the birth of Christ and it says in Matthew 2:1 that Jesus was born in the days of Herod, you know he is writing this narrative as a continuation of what had come before. For Jesus to be born in these days of Herod might have been the worst possible time for a new king of Israel to be born. But Matthew is framing his book not as a tidy biography of Jesus but as the clash of kingdoms.

Russell Moore urges us to remember that "Jesus was not born into a gauzy, snowy 'winter wonderland' of sweetly-singing angels and cute reindeer nuzzling one another at the side of his manger. He was born into a warzone. Jesus was chased out of his manger and into Egypt by . . . King Herod, who also sacrificed Bethlehem's infant children for the sake of power."[2]

✦ Who Is Herod? ✦

So who exactly is King Herod? He is the Roman-appointed governor of Judea, who took office in around 40 BC. He is known as Herod the Great because he was a builder, constructing impressive water systems known as aqueducts and rebuilding Solomon's Temple.

Herod's architectural achievements are impressive and some still exist today. I've walked among the aqueducts and have visited portions of the temple that still stand today in Israel. But Herod was also ruthless and paranoid. All of Israel knew he was not a legitimate king of Israel, having descended from Esau. So he ruled by fear. Here is just a short list of some of his violent acts:

✦ Herod killed the final members of the Hasmonean ruling family.

✦ Herod had many of the members of the Sanhedrin executed.

✦ Herod slaughtered members of his own family: his wife Mariamne, his mother-in-law Alexandra, and three of his sons.

✦ Herod even tried to have all the elite leaders in Jerusalem killed upon his death, arranging for them to be herded into the hippodrome and killed the moment he passed. This last decree of violence was ignored.[3]

So imagine how bothered Herod might be when a noisy entourage arrives from the East asking, naively, about a new king of the Jews. Matthew says, all of Jerusalem "was disturbed" (Matt. 2:3 NIV). The people were disturbed because the king was disturbed. And this was no mere annoyance. This was a culture of fear. Word got quickly back to Herod, who sprang into action. Not because he wanted, as he claimed, to worship the infant Jesus. In this baby, the evil king saw a threat to his power.

Herod gathered all of the religious people: the scribes and the scholars. These people knew the law backward and forward. And interestingly, they knew exactly what the prophets predicted. They even quoted from Micah 5:2:

> . . . and assembling all the chief priests and scribes of the people, he inquired of them where the Christ was to be born. They told him, "In Bethlehem of Judea, for so it is written by the prophet . . ." (Matt. 2:4–5)

So Herod summons the magi. He's clearly paranoid and is about to execute a plan to quash this insurrection, even if that threat was in diapers in Bethlehem.

Watch closely how Herod employs seemingly spiritual, benevolent language. He even uses the language of worship. It's a reminder to us how easily powerful people co-opt religious language to manipulate and destroy.

✦ The Real King of Judah ✦

Herod had his plan, but it turns out that he was not as powerful as he thought. Like every ruler who seeks to challenge God, his attempts to snuff out of the life of the real King of Israel were thwarted by God. God warned the wise men not to report back to Herod, and He warned Joseph to travel with Mary and the infant Jesus to Egypt for safety. This is a reminder, in a world of evil and suffering, when it seems that Satan has the upper hand, that God is sovereign over all things. In Psalm 2, David described God's response to the nations and rulers who plot against the Almighty:

> *Why do the nations rage*
> *and the peoples plot in vain?*
> *The kings of the earth set themselves,*
> *and the rulers take counsel together,*
> *against the LORD and against his Anointed, saying,*
> *"Let us burst their bonds apart*
> *and cast away their cords from us."*
> *He who sits in the heavens laughs;*
> *the Lord holds them in derision.*
> *Then he will speak to them in his wrath,*
> *and terrify them in his fury, saying,*
> *"As for me, I have set my King*
> *on Zion, my holy hill."*
> *(2:1–6)*

This is the story of Matthew's gospel, the story of Christmas: that God has determined to set upon His hill His King, Jesus. The earth is full of the graves of kings who tried and failed to usurp the true King, from Eden on through the life of Jesus. Herod may have seemed powerful. He may have initiated a culture of fear in Israel. But he was no match for the King of kings.

This is what we should take away from the life of Herod this Christmas: the people we think possess the most power, who put fear in our hearts, are really not that powerful. James Montgomery Boice says that "God is not troubled by this cosmic rebellion. God laughs at such folly."[4]

✦ Threatened by a Child ✦

This infant child, innocent and pure, now threatened the power center of Judea. Just imagine how angry Herod must have been when he failed to hear back from the wise men. Ghosted by the magi, he went into a rage and slaughtered every baby boy in Bethlehem under two years of age. In the most wicked kind of action, Herod saw children as a threat to his power and with cruel math—making sure no living infant son in Bethlehem could one day grow up and take his throne—he brought the sorrow of his sword into Jewish families.

Let's pause and just think of how much anguish this brought into the sleepy city of David. Families, having babies torn from their arms and taken by Herod's sword. As the father of four children, I can't even imagine watching one of my children dying, let alone like this.

And yet this is the way of tyrants, the way of people so consumed with power they cannot see the humanity of those in their way.

It was the way of Pharaoh, who murdered Jewish boys. And it's the way of so many monstrous acts of murder today. I still tear up when I think of the horrendous violence, several Christmases ago, in an elementary school in Connecticut. It still makes me shudder and weep to think of the massacre at Sandy Hook, how parents who dropped their children off at school one day—something millions of parents like me do every day—came home without that precious son or daughter. That Christmas in 2012 and every Christmas after, there are empty rooms, unopened Christmas gifts, and shattered hearts. As a father, every bit of anger wells up in me at the monster that caused this pain.

There is something about children that threatens evil people, Russell Moore says:

> Satan hates children because he hates Jesus. When evil destroys "the least of these" (Matt. 25:40, 45), the most vulnerable among us, it destroys a picture of Jesus himself, of the child delivered by the woman who crushes the head of our reptilian overlord (Gen. 3:15). The demonic powers know that the human race is saved, and they're vanquished, by a child born of woman (Gal. 4:4; 1 Tim. 2:15). And so they hate the children who bear his nature. . . .
>
> The satanic powers want the kingdoms of the universe, and a child uproots their reign.[5]

A child uproots their reign. And the uprooting by this child, Jesus, would signal the end of something. "Unto us a child is born, unto us a son is given," we read in Isaiah 9:6 (KJV). But this promise comes in the context of judgment against the evil powers. You see, a child, this child, threatens Herod and everyone who aligns against the Holy One. The child born in the manger was a sign of judgment. He is peace to those who put their trust in Him, but He is an enemy to those who wish to go their own way.

This judgment, though, is a sign of hope, of something new on the way. As Matthew narrates Herod's violence against the innocents, he quotes from Jeremiah 31 and echoes the weeping endured by a previous generation of Hebrew mothers and fathers, lamenting the loss of their land and the carrying of their children away to a foreign land. D. A. Carson explains why Matthew's inclusion of the passage is so important to our understanding:

> Jeremiah 31:15 occurs in a setting of hope. Despite the tears, God says, the exiles will return; and now Matthew, referring to Jeremiah 31:15, likewise says that, despite the tears of the Bethlehem mothers, there is hope because Messiah has escaped Herod and will ultimately reign. . . .
>
> . . . Matthew has already made the Exile a turning point in his thought (1:11–12), for at that time the Davidic line was dethroned. The tears of the Exile are now being "fulfilled"—i.e., the tears begun in Jeremiah's day are climaxed and ended by the tears of the mothers of Bethlehem. The heir to David's throne has come, the Exile is over, the true Son of God has arrived—and he will introduce the new covenant (26:28) promised by Jeremiah.[6]

The heir to David's throne has come. The long cosmic struggle between the seed of the serpent and the seed of the woman has culminated in Christ. Satan, the father of lies, the author of bloodshed, with murder on his heart, will be defeated when this baby ascends to a bloody Roman cross, endures the wrath of the Father, and rises again in victory on the third day. And the sin that has so gripped human hearts is being rolled back. This, Christmas reminds us, is the true kingdom. Jesus' kingdom is not a kingdom that prizes power over the vulnerable, but is a kingdom of flourishing, where the last shall be first, a kingdom made up of the weak and the ignoble.

Matthew is not giving us a fake Christmas wrapped in bows of sentimentality. He's giving us something better: hope.

This doesn't make the suffering and the violence and the bloodshed any less evil or hard to endure. Matthew is not giving us a fake Christmas, wrapped in bows of sentimentality. He's giving us something better: hope.

So at Christmas, as we survey the brokenness of our world and of the world Jesus entered, we should avoid two wrong approaches. We should be tempted away from an overly optimistic, Pollyannaish disposition that refuses to acknowledge evil; and it should keep us from a despair that only sees violence and horror. In Jesus, we see both the crying of Rachel for her children and the promise that those tears are being wiped away in a new and lasting kingdom of God. We see a weeping heavenly Father and a triumphant Christ.

As if to punctuate this hope, Matthew includes this little note: "But when Herod died . . ." (2:19). Herod, the paranoid and powerful monarch, died. And what's more, his kingdom was divided up by Rome, his sons sharing some of the power. And not too many decades later, there would be no more Herods at all on the throne of Israel. But that infant Herod tried to kill? He lives forever, having defeated sin, death, and the grave. The infant King would outlast the illegitimate king. The seed of the woman would crush the head of Satan.

And it is this hope that is carried by the people of God in every age. When we gather on Sundays, when we talk about Jesus to our friends and neighbors. When we work and when we play. We do all of this with this kingdom expectation: we are the ones who can look evil in the face and say to ourselves and to the world that a new day is dawning. And we can read the headlines, not with apathetic indifference or trembling fear, but with confidence that the kingdom of God is on the move, as the great hymn "A Mighty Fortress Is Our God" proclaims:

And though this world, with devils filled,
Should threaten to undo us,
We will not fear, for God has willed
His truth to triumph through us:
The prince of darkness grim,
We tremble not for him;
His rage we can endure,
For lo! his doom is sure;
One little word shall fell him.

✦ **The Herod Inside** ✦

There is also a personal lesson we should learn from the life of Herod this Christmas. Most of us, when reading the Christmas story in Matthew, like to fashion ourselves as the good guys. We'd be the wise men, rushing to worship Jesus. Or we'd be the shepherds declaring the good news. Or we'd be Simeon and Anna, waiting with anticipation for Jesus.

But it could be that there is more Herod in us than we want to admit. We too are threatened by Jesus, the way He enters ours lives and disrupts our power.

King Herod's reaction to Christ is, in this sense, a picture of us all. If you want to be king, and someone else comes along saying he is the king, then one of you has to give in. Only one person can sit on an absolute throne. . . . It is a claim of absolute authority, a summons to unconditional loyalty, and it inevitably triggers deep resistance within the human heart. . . . This dark episode of King Herod's violent lust for power points to our natural resistance to, even hatred of, the claims of God on our lives. We create Gods of our liking to mask our own hostility to the real God, who reveals himself as our absolute King.[7]

It's easy for us to point to the tyrants who ruled in Jesus' day and in our day, whispering silent prayers of relief that we are not they. But we may miss the Herod in our own hearts, the ways in which we resist the way of Jesus in favor of our own pursuits, how we quickly put trust in worldly powers instead of grounding our hope in the kingdom of God, how easy it is to marginalize "the little people" who seem to get in our way.

Herod also serves as a powerful reminder that we cannot be neutral about Jesus. We can either take up arms against Him—or we can bow down and worship in repentance and faith.

REFLECTION QUESTIONS:

1. *Take some time to write down and trace the cosmic battle between God and Satan, from Genesis 3 through the life of Jesus.*
   a. *How does this perspective change the way you see the Bible fitting together as one story?*
   b. *How does this help you make sense of evil in the world?*

2. *Reread Jeremiah 31.* Think through how this helps us understand Matthew's quotation of this prophetic passage and how it offers genuine Christian hope.

3. *Meditate on the ways in which we are tempted to yield to the Herod impulses in all of us:*
   a. *How we are tempted to step on the "little people" in order to gain power.*
   b. *How we are tempted to marginalize those who get in our way.*
   c. *How we resist the rule of Christ over our lives.*

SUGGESTED CHRISTMAS SONG:

"The Slaughter of Innocents" performed by The Waverly Consort

CHAPTER NINE

The Oldest Bucket List: Simeon and Anna

Luke 2:21–38

Lord, now you are letting your servant depart in peace,
according to your word; for my eyes have seen your salvation
that you have prepared in the presence of all peoples, a light
for revelation to the Gentiles, and for glory to your people Israel.

LUKE 2:29–32

At the tender young age of ninety, the late President George H. W. Bush strapped himself to Sgt. First Class Mike Elliot, a member of the Army's Golden Knights parachute team, and jumped out of an airplane near his summer home in Kennebunkport, Maine.

Bush, a former World War II fighter pilot, was fulfilling a series of promises he had made to himself—this one a vow to go skydiving in his nineties. This jump was made a bit easier. After all, he was a veteran skydiver after taking the leap at ages eighty and eighty-five!

If you are reading this today with your coffee or hot chocolate, you are probably not dreaming of falling out of an airplane at a ridiculously high altitude, on purpose. I certainly am not. But if I were to ask you, you probably do have your own set of crazy dreams you'd like to see fulfilled by the time you leave this earth.

Like President Bush, we all have a bucket list. Since the 2007 movie starring Morgan Freeman and Jack Nicholson, this idea of a list of high-value experiences, to be experienced before we "kick the bucket," has become part of our cultural lingo.

Some would like to climb Mt. Everest.

Some would like to find true love and get married.

Some would like to go skydiving.

Some would like to meet a famous person.

I'll admit that my list is a bit more pedestrian. I'd like to meet a few former presidents, I'd like to take a six-month trek across Europe with my wife, and I wouldn't mind preaching in a famous pulpit.

Okay, a Porsche wouldn't be bad either.

In the first century, they didn't call it a bucket list and Morgan Freeman wasn't there to narrate the high jinks, but the same poignant desires that inspire these dreams were present in human hearts. And in the Christmas story, Luke records the longings of two otherwise ordinary people.

✦ A Common Ceremony ✦

Simeon and Anna make their cameo at an otherwise common Jewish purification ritual. Today we put Mary and Joseph in klieg lights, and they adorn our nativity sets and Christmas cards. But in this first century, Luke peels back the curtain on an otherwise ordinary day. No spotlights. No press releases. No TV coverage.

To outside observers, Mary and Joseph were just another Jewish family showing up at the temple for the purification rite. They were following the Jewish law. Seven days after birth, Jesus was circumcised, and thirty-three days after circumcision, Mary and Jesus were back here in the temple for the purification ceremony and the presentation of their child to the Lord for His service.

But here is where this moment is anything but ordinary. That baby, after all, is the Son of God, the One whose words breathed out creation, sculpted Adam and Eve from the dust of the ground, and breathed into His own parents the breath of life. He was publicly identifying with His people, Israel, by submitting to the circumcision. Jesus, perfectly submitting to the Law that only He could perfectly fulfill,

Nobody in the temple that day was looking for a Savior.

the spotless One identifying with the impure so that Mary, Joseph, Simeon, Anna, and all true believers might one day become pure.

Mary and Joseph carried with them two turtledoves as part of the sacrifice offering. There is, of course, deep irony here. Though they carried in their arms the Lamb of God, they were too poor to purchase a lamb and instead, had to settle for the lesser turtledoves. It reminds us of the kind of people among whom God chose to dwell. The kingdom of Christ breaks in, not in the palaces or private estates of the powerful, but among the common, the meek, the kind of people who had to dig for enough shekels to afford turtledoves. And the baby held so tightly in their arms would one day become the perfect sacrifice for sins that these slain animals symbolized, the Lamb of God slain for the sins of the world.

+ A People Who Were Ready +

But here's the thing. Nobody in the temple that day was looking for a Christ child. Nobody was seeking a Savior. Nobody expected, on this of all days, a moment that would be written down later in ink by a doctor and preserved as Scripture for us to read today. There was a heaviness in Jerusalem that day, and most days. It had been centuries since God had spoken directly to His people. And every time Jewish people trudged past their temple, they had to see the Roman flag, flying high above their land, a visual slap in the face reminding them of their lost glory.

Would-be messiahs had come and gone. Now they were ruled by men like Herod, whose corrupt ascension to power and ruthless leadership further disillusioned ordinary Jews. None of them thought the solution for the corruption in Rome and the malfeasance in Herod's palace and the sin in their own hearts was resting, not a few feet away, in a carpenter's arms.

Even the religious elites in this temple, who pored over the ancient books and prided themselves on knowing every last arcane point of theology, were oblivious to Jesus.

But among the crowds that day, not among the waiting parents, not among the religious leaders, was a mysterious old man and a mysterious old woman. Unlike their peers, unlike the cynics, unlike the religious leaders, Anna and Simeon held on to a seemingly impossible wish grounded in a radical faith in the Scriptures' promise of a coming Messiah. Would God appear in the flesh in their day?

Though most missed the signs and the prophecies and the star. Though many dismissed the frenzied tales of those shepherds. Though even the authorities ignored the searching of the traveling Eastern mystics, Anna and Simeon waited and believed.

They studied the Scriptures and the prophecies. But more than that, they listened to the voice of God's Spirit.

✦ Who Is Simeon? ✦

So who is this Simeon character who just kind of appears from the shadows, into the gospel story? What's interesting is that two thousand years later, we still don't really know who he was. Luke, who wrote his eyewitness account with painstaking detail, thought only one thing mattered in Simeon's bio: "righteous and devout, waiting for the consolation of Israel."

We don't know anything about his family. We don't know what town he was born in. We don't even know his occupation. All the markers that we use to describe ourselves and those we befriend are gone. Only one thing mattered to Luke: Simeon was a faithful follower of Yahweh who, unlike those around him, still believed God would work to save His people.

Simeon believed the promise of a coming Servant-King, the son of David, threaded throughout the law and the prophets. He may not have understood everything he read, but he knew enough to believe. Simeon knew enough to listen to the Holy Spirit's whisper and was more in tune with God than the scholars who were paid to study and the scribes who were paid to teach.

Imagine the scene in the temple that day. An old man, stooped and graying, coming every day to the temple, expecting the Messiah. The religious people probably think he's an eccentric. They make jokes behind his back. *There's Simeon. He thinks the Lord is coming today!*

Every day he scans the crowd. Every day he asks the Lord, "Is this baby the one?" and every day the Lord says, "No, Simeon, this is not the one."

And then finally one day the Spirit of God whispers those words: *This is the day. This is the One. You will meet the Son of God.*

Perhaps he's reminded of the way Israel's last great king was chosen. A similarly aging man of faith approached Jesse's lineup of young men, asking the Lord, *Is this the next king?* And the Spirit answers Samuel, each time, *No, this isn't the one.* Until finally, David, the unlikely shepherd boy, summoned from the shepherds' fields, enters.

Yes, this is the next king of Israel.

Imagine how Simeon's aging heart leaped within him. "Can I hold your child?" he asks. And in his arms, Simeon carries the frail, newborn baby whose arms would one day carry Simeon from sin to salvation. He looks into the eyes of his tiny Savior, the same Jesus who holds up the universe with His power.

What wells up in Simeon's heart were words he had been preparing to share his entire life. A prayer that has been memorized, sung and framed from caves to cathedrals throughout church history:

> "Lord, now you are letting your servant depart in peace,
>   according to your word;
> for my eyes have seen your salvation
>   that you have prepared in the presence of all peoples,
> a light for revelation to the Gentiles,
>   and for glory to your people Israel."
> (Luke 2:29–32)

I can die because I've seen Your salvation. This, for Simeon, was no ordinary baby. He would not only be Simeon's salvation, but the salvation of the world, people from every nation, tribe, and tongue. This is the One of whom God spoke to Abraham, when He promised that the patriarch's heir would bless the nations. This is the One of whom God spoke to David when He promised the monarch an everlasting kingdom. This is the One of whom the prophets spoke, a Lion of the tribe of Judah, a suffering Servant, a conquering King.

Simeon had met Jesus, and Simeon was ready to die.

Death, of course, is a strange subject for Christmas. It doesn't make for heartwarming holiday entertainment. But Simeon knew he could face death—something every one of us will face one day—because he met the One who would conquer death.

There is so much for us to learn from Simeon's life. His perseverance, his attentive listening to God in a cynical age, his worship of the baby Jesus. But what is most important about Simeon—and you—was his relationship with Jesus. Simeon could die, not because he checked off the right religious boxes or performed all the outward rituals of the Jewish faith, but because he put his faith in the God-man.

As you read this, I can't help but wonder and hope that you, too, have peace with God. You, like Simeon, can be unafraid of death because you can know and understand that this baby is the triumphant, conquering Jesus whose own death and resurrection defeated sin, death, and the grave.

Don't misunderstand: Simeon wasn't seeking death. And neither should we. But there is a sweet assurance in knowing that if and when our time comes, whether tomorrow or in forty years, we can face death with peace because we know the Prince of Peace.

In my experience as a pastor, the people who were most full of life, who walked through every day with joy and verve, were those who were most at peace with their own mortality, who understood that this little baby in the manger we celebrate at Christmas defeated the grave. This is why Paul could say, of his own contentment, "to live is Christ, and to die is gain" (Phil. 1:21). Either way, he has peace and Christ is glorified.

This is the central message of Christmas. No doubt today as you read this, you are enveloped in the warmth and busyness of another December. But as much as we enjoy the season, let us remember that we set aside time, as believers, not merely to gather with family or to sip warm beverages, but to acknowledge the central truth of Christianity: Jesus has come to save us from our sins.

Sometimes we are tempted to think Jesus came only to save people who look like us.

This Jesus, Simeon knew, wasn't just an ordinary baby. He may not have understood exactly how it would all play out, nor did he fully grasp the mystery of God becoming human (neither do we). But Simeon knew enough to know that Jesus would not only be the long-awaited Messiah every Jewish person longed to see; He would be "a light for the Gentiles." This is repeated, often, in the gospel narratives of Jesus' birth. In Mary's song. In Zechariah's praise. In the words of the angel to Joseph.

Jesus was and is a Savior for the entire world. It's important for us to understand this truth. Sometimes we are tempted to think Jesus came only to save people who look like us, but we are told, from the promise to Abraham in Genesis through the words of the prophets and on into the gospel narratives and on through the letters of Paul and into John's vision in Revelation, that the kingdom of God is made up of people from every nation, tribe, and tongue.

And let's not forget the great cost of our salvation. This day in the temple was a day of celebration and dedication, but Simeon's words were not all pleasant for Mary to hear, especially his proclamation that "a sword will pierce" her soul. This is not what new mothers exactly want to hear about their motherhood, but Simeon knew that the promise carried joy and pain, blessing and anguish. The baby whom Simeon held, who cooed and kicked and delighted his young parents, would one day endure the unjust trial, motivated by bloodthirsty crowds. The very people He formed as Creator would laugh at His cries of pain. The world He came to save would send Him to His death. Most of all, the Father with whom He communed in all of eternity would see His Son not as the pure and spotless Lamb, but as the embodiment of all the sin and anguish of a rebellious human race.

This sword was Mary's unique calling. One day she would kneel at the foot of an ugly Roman instrument of execution: a cross. One day she would weep, with the others, as He lay dead in a borrowed tomb. One day she would question and fear and doubt the angel's promise.

Simeon's word to Mary was rooted in the prophet's vision of a coming King who would both suffer and conquer, who would reign over His enemies and yet be pierced for the transgressions of His people. This is why Christmas is both wonderful and yet violent, far from the saccharine holiday we often celebrate. The kingdom of God was to first come through the violent death of the Son of God.

But Mary, like all of those who believe, could find hope that the baby she held would not only pay for the sins of those who nailed

Him to the cross, but would defeat death in His resurrection. Her son would endure all of this to reconcile sinners—like herself, like Simeon, like you and me—and God. Jesus' future agony would be our salvation and God's glory.

✦ The First Evangelist ✦

Simeon was joined in his longing by another pilgrim. Like Simeon, we don't know much about Anna other than she was a prophetess from the tribe of Asher. A prophetess is simply Luke's way of telling us that she was gifted and unafraid to declare the word of the Lord. When we think of a prophetic word, we often think of predictions. But for Anna, it seems her most important ministry was to show up at the temple and remind God's people of God's words of promise and hope.

When I think of Anna, I think of a kind of steadfast courage. Here she is, a widow for much of her life, clinging to a distant promise, declaring good news to people worn out and weary. And she did this every day, for years.

Anna's presence here helps understand the upside-down nature of God's kingdom. In an age of celebrity, we assume that God is mostly at work among the famous and gifted, that the church is built on the gifts of those with the biggest social media following or largest congregations. But the church mostly advances along through the winding paths of the ordinary and the outcasts, the misfits and the forgotten.

You'll notice that the nativity does contain some nobles like the magi, but most of those around Jesus were simple and otherwise ordinary.

Luke tells us that Anna was a constant presence at the temple. She fasted day and night, longing in anticipation for the Messiah. Anna had her eyes fixed on God and was in attendance for the presentation of the Son of God.

This tells us the kinds of people whom God visits: those who wait for Him, day and night.

STUDY REFLECTIONS:

As we look at the lives of Anna and Simeon, we learn powerful messages for our own lives. If you are reading this with a group, you may want to gather together and consider that . . .

1. ***God visits the humble.*** The other name for Jesus, Immanuel, means "God with us." You see, we know a God who is with us. He visits us in our low estate. As you read the Christmas story, you see the people God chose to visit: lowly shepherds, foreign dignitaries, ordinary laypeople, a peasant couple, and a widow from the tribe of Asher. These are the people God uses. And so we can find ourselves in the story. God is with us. He's not just with the mighty and the powerful. God is with us.

   a. *What are you doing to prepare your heart for Jesus?*

   b. *What titles, honors, or glory are keeping you from a humble and contrite heart this Christmas?*

2. ***We too should faithfully anticipate the coming of Jesus.*** Just as Anna and Simeon faithfully anticipated the coming of Jesus, against all odds, against the logic of the times and the skepticism of the age, so should we cling to the hope of Jesus' Second Coming. I imagine that in their day people said, "Give it up, He's not coming." And yet they held out faith, and so should we. People say to me, "He's not coming.

They've been saying that for years." And yet He is coming, and we wait and believe.

a. *Has your heart grown cold to the story of Jesus' coming because of sin in the church and brokenness in the world?*

b. *Is it time to lean in again on the promise of Jesus, who not only fulfilled the promise in His first coming, but has promised to come again in victory?*

3. **Are you ready to die?** This sounds like a morbid question, but it's really a hopeful question. Can we, like Anna and Simeon, find peace with God? They saw the Messiah and could pass into eternity. And if you're ready to die, you're ready to live.

a. *Have you had a personal encounter with the Jesus of Scripture? Is it time to repent of your sins and follow Jesus as Lord and Savior?*

b. *Perhaps you are a follower of Jesus, but you've let your heart grow cold toward Him. Are there sins you need to confess in order to renew your walk with Him?*

4. **What's on your bucket list?** For Simeon it was to see Jesus. For the apostle Paul, his only goal was to know Christ more. Is that yours? Paul also said he wanted to stay here and share the good news or go to heaven and be with Christ.

a. *What items are on your spiritual bucket list?*

b. *Are there any areas of your life that have become idols, more important than knowing Jesus?*

SUGGESTED CHRISTMAS SONG:

Isaac Watts's Christmas hymn: "The King of Glory Sends His Son"

CHAPTER TEN

The Surprising People in Jesus' Family

Matthew 1:1–11

*The book of the genealogy of Jesus Christ,
the son of David, the son of Abraham.*

MATTHEW 1:1

I'm a Junior. My name is Daniel Michael Darling Jr. My dad is Daniel Michael Darling Sr." This is something my ten-year-old son proudly shares almost every time someone asks him his name. It's a bit sobering for me as well. Having given my son my name, I have to live in such a way that bearing that name won't be a major embarrassment for him throughout his life.

Naming our children is one of the most precious gifts God gives parents. We have four children. Besides my son, we have three girls, two of whom were born around Christmastime. This time of year we are not only celebrating the birth of Jesus, we are celebrating the birth of Emma and Grace.

Though we, like many parents, agonized over the names of our children, we don't invest as much significance in this practice as parents did in Jesus' day. Throughout the Bible, names were weighted with importance, signaling not only the type of person that soul would be, but signaling to whom you belonged.

Today there is a renewed interest in genealogy, motivated perhaps by the way the internet has made it easier to trace our family histories. Services like 23andMe and AncestryDNA have people around the world finding new relatives and discovering their full ethnic identities.

Matthew begins his gospel—and thus the beginning of the Christmas story—with a list of names. This is the part most of us likely skip when doing our Bible reading. Rarely does a public reading of Scripture include these, and few pastors preach whole sermons on a seemingly boring registry.

But Matthew didn't put this list in here because he needed to pad the page count of his gospel. He was making a bold statement about who Jesus is.

14 x 3 = Jesus

Matthew opens his gospel by making an audacious claim:

The book of the genealogy of Jesus Christ, the son of David, the son of Abraham. (1:1)

Matthew is telling his readers that this itinerant rabbi from Nazareth arrested on false charges and executed by the Romans, Joseph's son, is the rightful Heir to the throne of David and thus, the promised Son of God. And to use today's language, he has the receipts to prove it.

He begins, first, by mentioning two important names. Jesus, he says, is the son of David and the son of Abraham. Why does this matter? To fully understand this, we have to go back to Genesis.

When God called Abraham to leave his family and everything

familiar to go to a place he didn't know, this wasn't because God was interested in Abraham becoming a wandering muse. God was doing something with Abraham. From this once-pagan man would come a family and from this family a nation. This is what God promised him numerous times:

> *Now the LORD said to Abram, "Go from your country and your kindred and your father's house to the land that I will show you. And I will make of you a great nation, and I will bless you and make your name great, so that you will be a blessing. I will bless those who bless you, and him who dishonors you I will curse, and in you all the families of the earth shall be blessed." (Gen. 12:1–3)*

> *And he brought him outside and said, "Look toward heaven, and number the stars, if you are able to number them." Then he said to him, "So shall your offspring be." And he believed the LORD, and he counted it to him as righteousness. (Gen. 15:5–6)*

It was incomprehensible at the time for Abraham to ponder how God would make, from his family, a nation, and not just any nation, but a people that would bless "all the families on the earth." How in the world would this be possible? And yet this promise was repeated to Isaac (Gen. 26) and to Jacob (Gen. 28) and through the generations of the people of Israel.

Later in Israel's history, God would pluck another man from obscurity and make an even bigger and seemingly impossible promise. He urged Samuel to find David from the shepherd fields and anoint him as Israel's next king, and when David did finally assume the throne of Israel, God said He would preserve the throne of David, *forever*:

"When your days are fulfilled and you lie down with your fathers,
I will raise up your offspring after you, who shall come from your
body, and I will establish his kingdom. He shall build a house for my
name, and I will establish the throne of his kingdom forever. I will
be to him a father, and he shall be to me a son. When he commits
iniquity, I will discipline him with the rod of men, with the stripes
of the sons of men, but my steadfast love will not depart from him,
as I took it from Saul, whom I put away from before you. And your
house and your kingdom shall be made sure forever before me. Your
throne shall be established forever." (2 Sam. 7:12–16)

A kingdom, forever? Think about how this must have sounded
to David. Sure, as a monarch, he wanted his son to reign and his son's
son to reign and for the line of succession to continue. But even the
most narcissistic rulers, who hear "O king, live forever," don't usually
believe it. How do you ensure that your family is in power forever?

But this was not hyperbole. God really meant it and renewed this
promise even after the kingdom of Israel was divided and conquered
and centuries after David died and was buried. Here is one such promise: "And I will set up over them one shepherd, my servant David,
and he shall feed them: he shall feed them and be their shepherd. And
I, the LORD, will be their God, and my servant David shall be prince
among them. I am the LORD; I have spoken" (Ezek. 34:23–24).

This is the prophet Ezekiel, who was writing to a people who no
longer had possession of their land, who were ruled by another conquering kingdom, a people whose idolatry had invited the judgment
of God. And yet God continues to remind and renew His promise
made to David back in 2 Samuel 7.

This is just one example. If you take some time to read through the prophets (an exercise that will greatly strengthen your faith), you will see the name David mentioned over and over again, not in the past tense, as if in memorial, but as part of the future in God's redemptive plan. Can I share just one more of these promises, if you'll indulge me? Here is Jeremiah, often called the "weeping prophet" because of his dire predictions of God's judgment on a disobedient people. In the midst of the not so good, very bad news he had to deliver, he paused and recited anew this hope that a new David would come:

> *"Behold, the days are coming, declares the LORD, when I will raise up for David a righteous Branch, and he shall reign as king and deal wisely, and shall execute justice and righteousness in the land."* (Jer. 23:5)

The days are coming.

And Matthew is asserting in his gospel, with his opening list of hard-to-pronounce names, that this day has come.

The genealogy of Jesus Christ, the son of David, the son of Abraham.

Matthew is saying that Jesus is the fulfillment of God's promise to Abraham and Jesus is the new David, promised by the prophets. In this genealogy, Matthew traces Jesus' legal right to the throne of Israel through Joseph's line. In Luke 3, we see Jesus' lineage as traced through Mary's family. Both families come from the family of David, Joseph from Solomon's family and Mary from David's son Nathan. Luke traces Jesus back to Adam, to make the important case that Jesus is fully human and that He is the second Adam, come to reverse the curse and rescue humanity.

Matthew is making the case that Jesus is the fulfillment of the promise to David. In fact, even the way he arranges this list of names is significant, something we don't always pick up when we read our English translations of the Bible.

Notice what he is doing, in verse 17, when he divides his list into three lists of fourteen generations: Abraham to David, David until the exile, and the exile until Jesus. Matthew didn't include every single generation from Adam to Jesus in this genealogy. Instead, his use of fourteen generations, three times, had a specific purpose. The Hebrew language had a device called *gematria* that used letters as numbers.[1] So the consonants in every Hebrew word would add up to a number. David's names add up to the number fourteen (D=4, V=6, D=4).[2] So Matthew deliberately repeated this three times, as if to emphasize Jesus as the new David. What's more, David's name appears as the fourteenth name in this genealogy.

Matthew wasn't trying to be cute here. He was deliberately creating a way for faithful Jewish people to easily remember that Jesus Christ was a son of David. And it's not just that He's any son of David. Plenty of men came along who had the right family heritage, but Matthew says this Jesus is *the Christ*. The title Christ means Messiah or Anointed One.

Jesus, *the* son of Abraham, *the* son of David, *the* Christ. Why is this important? Because everything we celebrate at Christmas hinges on it. If this baby born in Bethlehem to peasant parents, who lived a perfectly sinless life, went to die on a Roman cross, and rose again on the third day, is indeed *the* Christ, then it changes everything.

It means Christmas is more than Hallmark movies and trips to Grandma's house, but is the celebration of the birth of the Son of God, the long-promised Messiah. It's the in-breaking of the kingdom of God. That's why it is important for us not to get caught up simply in the sentimentality of Christmas without realizing what it is we are celebrating. As my friend Dean Inserra says, "Sadly, in the name of tradition and good tidings . . . Christians can have all the comforts of the Christmas season without being confronted with their need to follow the very One whose birth they acknowledge." Dean says that it should be Christians who should be "responding to Christmas year round if we really do believe the words of the carols and the world-altering significance of the nativity scene."[3]

This really is the answer to the question: What does Christmas mean for me? Because if you are in Jesus, this story from Adam to Abraham, from David to Christ, is your story. And if you are not a follower of Jesus, if you have not repented of your sins and put your full faith in Jesus' death and resurrection, this can be your story. Because this same Jesus is today calling people from every nation, tribe, and tongue.

✦ A Messy Family ✦

Of course, by now as you look at Jesus' family tree, outlined in Matthew and Luke, you've got a few questions. Yes, it's awesome that Jesus is the new David, the son of Abraham, the promised Messiah, but what are all of these . . . misfits doing here?

David? Sure, he was Israel's best king, but isn't he the one who committed adultery and arranged for his mistress's husband to be killed? Abraham? Sure, he went out on faith, but didn't he lie about his wife? Didn't he have a child with his handmaid? And of all the sons of Jacob, did Jesus have to come from the family of . . . Judah? Have you read what Judah did? Selling his brother Joseph to traffickers. Sleeping with his daughter-in-law?

If you signed up for AncestryDNA and found out these people were in your family tree, I don't know that you'd tell anyone. "Hey honey, I just found out I'm related to a lying adulterer and murderer." It would be like discovering you were the great-grandson of the Boston Strangler or Benedict Arnold's long-lost fourth cousin.

The kind of people Jesus has in His family tree are infamous, not the kind of characters you'd put on your refrigerator. And yet . . . in this list of names is another, countercultural message. These are the kinds of people who make up the family of God. His kingdom, Jesus would remind us, would be the place where the last in line when it comes to holiness would be first and where the sinners of this world would find refuge:

> *And the scribes of the Pharisees, when they saw that he was eating with sinners and tax collectors, said to his disciples, "Why does he eat with tax collectors and sinners?" And when Jesus heard it, he said to them, "Those who are well have no need of a physician, but those who are sick. I came not to call the righteous, but sinners."*
> *(Mark 2:16–17)*

This is good news, my friend. Because though we might pretend, especially this time of year, that we have it all together, we know that there are parts of our lives that we'd rather not see exposed to the light of day. We know we are sick. And even in His genealogy, Jesus is telling us the kinds of people who are eligible for His gospel. Tim Keller says, "The world has always despised people from the wrong places and with the wrong credentials. We are always trying to justify ourselves. We need desperately to feel superior to others. And everything about Jesus contradicts and opposes that impulse."[4]

Jesus has come for outsiders and the sinner, the downcast and the powerless. In a word, He has come for you.

Read on to meet some more surprising relatives of Jesus.

STUDY REFLECTIONS:

1. *Review the promises to Abraham and David listed in chapter 10.*

   a. *How does Christ fulfill the promise for Abraham to be "a father of many nations" (Gen. 17:5 KJV)?*

   b. *How does Christ fulfill the promise to David to ensure a forever kingdom?*

2. *Read through Matthew 1 and Luke 3.* *Write down some of the names you know from the Old Testament. Ask yourself:*

   a. *What does the inclusion of these names tell us about the gospel?*

   b. *What does this tell us about the way God thinks about ordinary people?*

   c. *What does this tell us about the way God "names" us as His children by faith in Christ?*

3. *What are ways that other religions conflict with the Christianity presented by Jesus' fulfillment of the promise as laid out in Matthew 1?*

   a. *What does the inclusion of sinners in the genealogy tell us about the gospel?*

   b. *How should that make us feel about ourselves—our own self-righteousness and ability to please God?*

4. *Go around the table with your family and spend some time discussing your own names—why you were named this way, what it means, etc.*

SUGGESTED CHRISTMAS SONG:

Francesca Battistelli, "He Knows My Name"

CHAPTER ELEVEN

The Even More Surprising People in Jesus' Family

To close out this Christmas journey, I'd like to highlight four characters from Jesus' family tree that illustrate the upside-down nature of the kingdom of God. All of them are women, which is remarkable in and of itself.

Typically, Jewish genealogies didn't mention women. They only ever listed men as the heads of their households. Women in the ancient world had little agency and had virtually no voice. So in telling the Christmas story through women like Mary and Elizabeth and Anna, Jesus is telling us that His kingdom is a different kind of kingdom. And even in this small and seemingly insignificant detail of listing four women in Jesus' family tree, Matthew is communicating something powerful.

To fully grasp this, we have to understand how poorly women were regarded in the first century. A woman had no legal rights and was completely subject to her husband's power. According to New Testament scholar Michael Green, a Jewish man "thanked God each day that he had not been created a slave, a Gentile, or a woman."[1]

To put it bluntly: it would be scandalous for Matthew to put these women's names in here. And these weren't just any women. Each one of them carried with them a stigma, an asterisk next to their name every time a faithful Jewish person heard their name read out loud in the temple or the synagogue.

✦ The Forgotten ✦

Tamar is a name most Jewish people likely wanted to forget. And yet here she is, in Genesis 38, first as the wife of a man named Er, one of two sons of Judah. These sons were the result of an adulterous relationship Judah had with another Canaanite woman. Er was not a good husband and was killed by God. When he died it was, according to custom at the time, for his next oldest brother, Onan, to marry Tamar and continue the family line. But in a greedy attempt to set himself up for a richer inheritance, he refused to conceive a baby with Tamar. As a result, God struck Onan dead as well.

The next brother was much younger, so Tamar waited and waited for Judah to give his youngest son as her husband. This never happened. Judah was reluctant, believing Tamar was somehow cursed by God. So she took things into her own hands and dressed up like a prostitute along a main roadway. Judah propositioned her and as a result of their liaison, they conceived. In an interesting twist, Judah, when he discovered she was pregnant, sought to put her to death for violating the oath to stay chaste until she remarried. But she proved to him that it was his children she bore. And yet, one of their two sons, Perez, would be an ancestor of King David and, eventually, King Jesus.

Judah and Tamar's place in the family of Jesus shows us a kind of interesting juxtaposition between the powerful and the powerless.

Judah was the hypocritical leader who covered his sin, who exploited his daughter-in-law to satisfy his passions. Then there is Tamar, helpless and forgotten. In Jesus' new family, both the religious hypocrite and the exploited mistress find their need for grace.

✦ The Sinful ✦

Rahab's story is similarly sordid (Josh. 2:1–7). When the Jewish spies came in to scout out the land of Jericho, she was the one who hid them in her home and protected them from the prying eyes of the government police. She had heard of the miracles God had wrought with Israel in Egypt and in the wilderness and, unlike the rest of her country, turned to faith in Yahweh. But her profession, Joshua tells us, was as a prostitute. She sold herself for the pleasure of men.

We recoil even at that word *prostitute* but we should know that in ancient times this was often the only way for a vulnerable woman, without a family or husband, to survive. This doesn't justify her lifestyle, but it reminds us that she was exploited for her body. Because she provided critical intelligence that helped Israel defeat Jericho, she was given safe harbor in Israel and grafted into the Jewish nation (Heb. 11:31). James, the brother of Jesus, says that her actions were evidence of her newfound faith (James 2:25).

Rahab's life is evidence that Jesus is always bringing in outsiders, those seen by religious institutions as too damaged by exploitation and sin. As we gather this Christmas to worship, we are tempted to think of ourselves as more righteous than the Rahabs in our world, but in a sense, every human being is as unclean in God's eyes as a prostitute. Paul, once an observant, faithful Jew, recognizes that there is none righteous before God (Rom. 3:10) and saw himself as the "chief" of sinners (1 Tim. 1:15 KJV). But the good news is that Jesus, by His life and death and resurrection, is bringing Rahabs into His new family.

✦ The Exploited ✦

You probably don't need an introduction to Bathsheba's story (2 Sam. 11–12). Even if you don't know the Bible, you might know what happened when King David looked down from his rooftop at a naked Bathsheba as she bathed. It was the biggest scandal during the reign of Israel's greatest king. Most of us think of this story in terms of what it means for David. Often it is used as a sloppy apologetic for our own sin. *David sinned and still was a man after God's own heart. David was repentant, so when we are repentant we will find grace. God still used David as a leader after his sin.*

But let's think about Bathsheba. The Bible never really seems to bring judgment on her for her place in David's life. It's likely that when David summoned her from her home, she had little choice but to comply. If you are a woman in the ancient world and the king summons you, you obey. The story gets even more complicated when you realize that Bathsheba is the young granddaughter of one of David's closest advisors, Ahithophel (2 Sam. 11:3).

The magnitude of David's gross sin cannot be overstated. He exploited Bathsheba. He used his power to get from her what he wanted. And not only did this result in the death of Bathsheba's husband, it was one of the pivotal events that divided David's family, causing the death of one of David's children with Bathsheba and a catalyst for an ugly, father-against-son civil war.

Bathsheba's life was one of difficulty and sorrow. She was likely an unpopular, even despised, woman in Israel and in David's family. She suffered the loss of a son and became the wife of an unfaithful husband. And yet here she appears in Matthew's retelling of the story of Israel and the promise of the Redeemer. She is named by God. A victim of exploitation. And so it is that God sees and knows all of those who are often exploited and abused. In Jesus, the forgotten can find a new family and a new identity.

✦ The Outsider ✦

Perhaps the most scandalous name in Jesus' genealogy is Ruth. Unlike the other three women, she doesn't have the sexually sordid backstory and she isn't the victim of abuse. And yet to the Jewish person hearing Matthew's account, her appearance would be offensive. Why?

Like Rahab, Ruth wasn't Jewish. But not only was Ruth not Jewish, she was a Moabite. Moabites were not simply Gentiles, they were one of Israel's sworn enemies. They weren't even allowed to enter the worship gathering of Israel. They were idolaters who had refused to help Israel as they made their way from Egypt.

But a famine in Israel sent a Jewish family—Naomi and Elimelech and their two sons—to Moab to survive. Ruth's life was one of difficulty and sorrow. She saw her husband, her brother-in-law, and her father-in-law perish in Moab. When Naomi, her mother-in-law, sought to return to her homeland, Ruth chose to follow her and worship Naomi's God (Ruth 1:16). She eventually became the wife of Boaz and the great-grandmother of King David. The book of Ruth beautifully tells the story of Boaz as Ruth's kinsman-redeemer, the one with power and resources to rescue and protect the vulnerable. And her appearance here in the opening pages of Christmas reminds us that Jesus is the redeemer of those who are on the outside, who, like the Moabitess Ruth, were once alien to the courts of the Almighty and are now brought in as full participants of the grace of God.

✦ Your Name in the Family of God ✦

So hopefully, by now, you will never read the first chapter of Matthew the same way again. But more importantly, I hope that you understand that Jesus is more than just a name in the Bible. He is *the* son of Abraham. He is *the* son of David. He is *the* Christ.

I find it comforting that God names these four, otherwise forgotten, otherwise outsider women. He names the exploited, the forgotten, the powerless.

The world may forget your name, but you can be known and named by the One who is the "name that is above every name" (Phil. 2:8–11). What's more, Jesus can give you a new name. This is the real meaning of Christmas, that God is in the business of taking sinners like you and me and making us new creations, with new identities and a new purpose:

> *Therefore, if anyone is in Christ, he is a new creation. The old has passed away; behold, the new has come. All this is from God, who through Christ reconciled us to himself and gave us the ministry of reconciliation; that is, in Christ God was reconciling the world to himself, not counting their trespasses against them, and entrusting to us the message of reconciliation. (2 Cor. 5:17–19)*

I hope you understand, as you close this book, that if there is room in the family of God for Rahab and Tamar, Abraham and Jacob, Ruth and Bathsheba, David and Judah, there is room for you. Is there anything keeping you from embracing, by faith, this good news?

STUDY REFLECTIONS:

1. *The stories of Tamar, Ruth, Rahab, and Bathsheba—all part of Jesus' lineage—show us that "Jesus is always bringing in the outsider, those seen by religious institutions as too damaged by exploitation and sin."* Who are some "outsiders" that today's religious institutions might exclude?

2. *How can your family or circle of friends "bring in the outsider," even this Christmas?*

3. *What are ways that other religions conflict with the Christianity presented by Jesus' fulfillment of the promise as laid out in Matthew 1?*

   a. *What does the inclusion of sinners in the genealogy tell us about the gospel?*

   b. *How should that make us feel about ourselves—our own self-righteousness and ability to please God?*

4. *The Gospels are full of stories of women who were significant in Jesus' life and earthly ministry.* We have already met several of them in this book! Who are some other examples, and what can we learn from them?

Imagine Yourself . . .

Hopefully by now you've come to realize that all the characters of Christmas point not to themselves, but to the central figure in the Christmas narrative: Jesus, the One whose birth, life, death, and resurrection change everything. Reading about this supporting cast allows us to get a closer look at the One who is worthy of our worship.

And we too might imagine ourselves gathered around the manger, looking at the incarnation from their point of view. Writing this book was such a pleasure because it allowed me to do just that. I hope, as a final exercise, you might approach these few days before Christmas this way.

So imagine yourself as a young, vulnerable Jewish woman, about to marry a man she likely barely knew. Imagine the weight of the angels' words that her calling would not simply be to be a mother and a wife, but to bear the Son of God in her womb. Mary said yes to God, and her obedience shone in the tapestry of God's redemptive movement in history. Later her Son would say yes to the Father, sweating drops of blood, so that we might be able to say yes to salvation. As you look from Mary's perspective, worship the King who purchased your freedom—and in joyous response, say yes back to Him.

Imagine yourself as Joseph, an ordinary man in an otherwise ordinary village with an ordinary vocation. History has suddenly descended on him, with a pregnant wife, a watching community, and a providential God. He, like Mary, submitted to this hard and difficult life, fathering a son he didn't conceive and bearing shame he didn't deserve. Like Joseph, we can obey the Father wherever He leads, and trust that His will for us is greater than our own ambitions and dreams. Joseph's view of Christmas allows us to hold loosely our lives and offer ourselves up in service to our King.

We might ask ourselves, like Joseph and Mary, in what areas is God asking us to offer our yes, in what areas are we having a difficult time yielding control?

Or perhaps we wait and long for an answer, like Simeon and Anna. There they stood in the temple, year after year, waiting for the dawn of God's kingdom. And when Jesus arrived, they were ready to worship, ready to rejoice. As we look back at Jesus' first advent, we also, like these two worshipers, prepare our hearts to wait in humble anticipation for His second coming and, in the in-between, for a fresh work of God's Spirit in our hearts this season.

Or, like Zechariah, perhaps we've lived in the shadow of unfulfilled longings. Weary of God's silence, cynical about His promises, for us Christmas might seem more ritual than restoration, but it could be that God is wrapping His promise in mystery, forcing us to be quiet, to listen, and to hear Him speak over us.

We are all, of course, either shepherds or wise men. We are shepherds who hear afresh the announcement of the good news of Jesus' entrance into the world, and we too are compelled, by Christmas, to go and share with those who have not yet heard. Or we are outsiders to religion, traveling like the wise men from a far country, following a distant light toward Jesus. May this season of wandering and seeking find you finally home, at the feet of the One whose birth changes your trajectory and reorders your worship.

We are certainly not angels. But we might step back and consider their view, watching God create humans to love and to receive love and watching the divine plan of rescue unfold in the world, to see those made in His image bear the recipients of His grace. We might watch the Son of God submit to the vulnerabilities of human life and then move toward the cross in sacrifice for the sins of His people. The angels were there every step of the way, from the dawn of creation to the folding of grave clothes in triumph to the final battle over God's enemies. We are not angels, but we can bend our ear to hear the words the angels say: *Glory to God in the highest!*

Lastly, we, like the ignominious names in the list of God's family, can find a new name and a new family in this new creation of God: the church. For those who have no name, or whose name has been tarnished by sin, and for those who have been passed by, Jesus knows your name and can give you a new name.

ACKNOWLEDGMENTS

It really does take a village to make a book. Here is my village:

Drew Dyck: Thanks for always seeing promise in my writing, from the earliest days at *Leadership Journal* all the way up until that fateful day in the lobby of Moody Bible Institute downtown when we hatched up an idea of a book profiling the many characters in the Christmas narrative.

Betsey Newenhuyse: Your brilliant editing and warm touch helped make this manuscript sparkle. Grateful for the way you've served the church with your careful pen and love of words.

Erik Wolgemuth and the entire Wolgemuth team: Thank you for your patience in my many sudden book ideas and helping me shepherd them into publishing realities.

Moody Publishers: Thank you for giving me a platform to write. Every book contract is an undeserved gift. Thanks for this gift.

Gages Lake Bible Church, who first heard many of these ideas in rough form, years ago, as Christmas sermons: Thanks for giving me an environment that allowed me to grow as a pastor and leader and husband and father.

Daryl Crouch, my current pastor at Green Hill Church: Thanks for encouraging me to continue to write for the glory of God and the edifying of the church.

ERLC team: Thanks for putting up with my crankiness around a book deadline and for letting me close my door, sometimes, and write.

Trey Suey: Thanks for helping me with research.

Angela: Thanks for being an amazing wife and not just enduring more book deadlines but pushing me to keep writing when I'm discouraged. Also for giving me a few Saturdays hunched over a laptop and piles of books.

Grace, Daniel Jr, Emma, and Lily: Thanks for understanding those Saturdays with me staring at a screen and understanding that "Daddy is writing a book." You are the best kids in the world.

Most of all, thank You to God for giving me the opportunities and passion to write. I pray these words bring glory to You and show others the riches of Your love, as expressed in the gift of Jesus to us at Christmas.

N O T E S

Introduction: Jesus, the Grandest Story of All

1. Fleming Rutledge, *Advent: The Once and Future Coming of Jesus Christ* (Grand Rapids: Eerdmans, 2018), 385–86.

2. Martin Luther, "Sermon on the Afternoon of Christmas Day (1530)," in *Martin Luther's Basic Theological Writings* (Minneapolis: Fortress Press, 2012), 172.

Chapter One ✦ Joseph, the Unsung Hero of Christmas

1. Craig S. Keener, *Matthew* (Downers Grove, IL: InterVarsity Press, 1997), 61.

2. Douglas Sean O'Donnell and R. Kent Hughes, *Matthew: All Authority in Heaven and on Earth* (Wheaton, IL: Crossway, 2013), 41.

3. David Platt, *Christ-Centered Exposition Commentary: Exalting Jesus in Matthew* (Nashville: B&H, 2013), 25.

4. Keener, *Matthew*, 63.

5. Timothy Keller, *Hidden Christmas: The Surprising Truth Behind the Birth of Christ* (New York: Viking, 2016), 56.

6. Russell Moore, "Let's Stop Ignoring Joseph," December 20, 2011, https://www.russellmoore.com/2011/12/20/lets-stop-ignoring-joseph/.

Chapter Two ✦ A Christmas Miracle: Zechariah and Elizabeth

1. Fleming Rutledge, *Advent: The Once and Future Coming of Jesus Christ* (Grand Rapids: Eerdmans, 2018), 52.

2. *NIV Zondervan Study Bible*, ed. D. A. Carson (Grand Rapids: Zondervan, 2015), 2066.

3. R. Kent Hughes, *Luke (2 Volumes in 1 / ESV Edition): That You May Know the Truth* (Wheaton, IL: Crossway, 2014), 22.

4. Rutledge, *Advent*, 378.

Chapter Three ✦ Mary, the Simple Girl at the Center of Everything

1. R. Kent Hughes, "Christmas Is for the Poor and Humble," Crossway, December 16, 2015, https://crossway.org/articles/christmas-is-for-the-poor-and-humble/.

2. Fleming Rutledge, *Advent: The Once and Future Coming of Jesus Christ* (Grand Rapids: Eerdmans, 2018), 388.

Chapter Four ✦ The Song of the Angels

1. R. Kent Hughes, *Luke (2 Volumes in 1 / ESV Edition): That You May Know the Truth* (Wheaton, IL: Crossway, 2014), 90.

Chapter Five ✦ Room for Jesus: The Innkeeper

1. Arthur Just Jr. and Thomas C. Oden, *Ancient Christian Commentary on Scripture: Luke* (Downers Grove, IL: InterVarsity Press, 2003), 39–40.

2. Ibid.

3. Frederick Buechner, *The Hungering Dark* (Harper Collins, 1985), 13.

4. *Luke*, Ancient Christian Commentary on Scripture, New Testament vol. 3, ed. Arthur A. Just Jr. (Downers Grove, IL: InterVarsity Press, 2003), 36.

5. Ibid., 38.

Chapter Six ✦ The First to Know: Shepherds

1. J. Vernon McGee, "God Manifest in the Flesh," Christianity.com, accessed February 8, 2019, https://www.christianity.com/theology/god-manifest-in-the-flesh-11569482.html.

2. Ibid.

3. R. Kent Hughes, *Luke (2 Volumes in 1 / ESV Edition): That You May Know the Truth* (Wheaton, IL: Crossway, 2014), 91.

4. John Calvin, *Harmony of Matthew, Mark, Luke*, trans. William Pringle (Grand Rapids: Baker Book House, n.d.), 113.

5. Martin Luther, "Sermon on the Afternoon of Christmas Day (1530)," in *Martin Luther's Basic Theological Writings* (Minneapolis: Fortress Press, 2012), 172.

Chapter Seven ✦ Seeking and Finding: The Wise Men

1. *CSB Study Bible* (Nashville: Holman Bible Publishers, 2017), 1498.

2. *CSB Spurgeon Bible* (Nashville: Holman Bible Publishers, 2017), 1281.

3. Manlio Simonetti, ed., *Ancient Christian Commentary, Matthew 1–13*, vol. 1a (Downers Grove, IL: IVP Academic, 2001), 27.

4. Ibid.

5. Ibid.

6. David Platt, *Christ-Centered Exposition Commentary: Exalting Jesus in Matthew* (Nashville: B&H, 2013), 38.

Chapter Eight ✦ Herod, the Monster of Christmas

1. Portions of this chapter are adapted from the author's blog post "The Monster of Christmas," December 8, 2010, DanielDarling.com, https://www.danieldarling .com/2010/12/the-monster-of-christmas/.

2. Russell Moore, "Planned Parenthood Vs. Jesus Christ," RussellMoore.com, August 4, 2015, www.russellmoore.com/2015/08/04/planned-parenthood-vs-jesus-christ/.

3. Michael Green, *The Message of Matthew* (London: SPCK, 2014).

4. James Montgomery Boice, *The Gospel of Matthew: The King and His Kingdom,* An Expositional Commentary, vol. 1 (Grand Rapids: Baker Books, 2001), 43.

5. Russell Moore, "School Shootings and Spiritual Warfare," RussellMoore.com, December 14, 2012, https://www.russellmoore.com/2012/12/14/school-shootings-and-spiritual-warfare/.

6. D. A. Carson, *Matthew*, The Expositor's Bible Commentary, Tremper Longman III and David E. Garland, eds. (Grand Rapids: Zondervan Academic, 2017), 96.

7. Timothy Keller, *Hidden Christmas: The Surprising Truth Behind the Birth of Christ* (New York: Viking, 2016), 67–70.

Chapter Ten ✦ The Surprising People in Jesus' Family

1. David Platt, *Christ-Centered Exposition Commentary: Exalting Jesus in Matthew* (Nashville: B&H, 2013), 25.

2. *NIV Zondervan Study Bible,* ed. D. A. Carson (Grand Rapids: Zondervan, 2015), 1927.

3. Dean Inserra, *The Unsaved Christian: Reaching Cultural Christianity with the Gospel* (Chicago: Moody Publishers, 2019), 93.

4. Keller, *Hidden Christmas*, 74–75.

Chapter Eleven ✦ The Even More Surprising People in Jesus' Family

1. Michael Green, *The Message of Matthew* (London: SPCK, 2014), 58.

Daniel Darling is a prolific author and speaker who believes Christmas music should be sung all year round. He currently serves as vice president for communications for the Ethics & Religious Liberty Commission. Dan is the author of several books, including *iFaith, REAL, The Original Jesus,* and *The Dignity Revolution.*He is a columnist for *HomeLife* and a regular contributor to *In Touch Magazine, Christianity Today,* and The Gospel Coalition. Dan's op-eds have appeared in *USA Today,* CNN, *Washington Times, Time, Huffington Post, National Review, Washington Post,* and *First Things.* Dan has served churches in Illinois and Tennessee. He and his wife, Angela, have four children and reside in the Nashville area.

How to focus on Christ during Advent

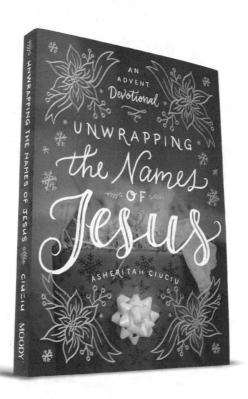

MOODY
Publishers

*From the Word **to** Life*

Unwrapping the Names of Jesus leads readers through the four weeks of Advent (Hope, Preparation, Joy, and Love) by focusing each day's reflection on one name of Jesus. Each week begins with an interactive family devotional followed by five daily reflections, as well as suggestions for fun-filled family activities or service projects to enhance a family's Advent experience.

978-0-8024-1672-8 | also available as an eBook

"We live between two *mighty events*"

— A. W. TOZER

Advent is as much about looking back as it is looking ahead—back to Christ's incarnation, ahead to His return. *From Heaven* combines A. W. Tozer's best reflections on these two themes to help us better appreciate the season of Advent.

MOODY
Publishers®

*From the Word **to** Life*®

978-1-60066-802-9 | also available as an eBook